UWEM ESSIA

STRATEGIC TAX PLANNING, ETHICAL EXCELLENCE, AND COMPLIANCE

Strategic Tax Management: Navigating Profits, Ethics, and Savings

This book was professionally typeset on Reedsy.
Find out more at reedsy.com

Dedicated to all the tax professionals, accountants, and financial planners whose unwavering integrity and commitment to ethical excellence shape the backbone of our financial systems. May this work serve as a guide and inspiration, illuminating the path toward strategic tax planning and compliance in an ever-evolving global landscape.

Contents

Preface

"Strategic Tax Planning, Ethical Excellence, and International Taxation Challenges" explores the multifaceted world of tax management, providing readers with an in-depth understanding of the complexities and intricacies involved. Chapter One explains the essence of strategic tax management, underscoring the critical balance between enhancing profitability and adhering to compliance. It emphasizes the importance of aligning tax-related decisions with a company's overarching financial goals, leveraging legal tax-saving opportunities without compromising ethical standards. The chapter further illustrates the importance of a well-structured corporate tax strategy and carefully managing taxable events to optimize tax positioning.

Chapter Two focuses on Base Erosion and Profit Shifting (BEPS), introducing readers to how multinational corporations navigate through different tax jurisdictions and highlighting the challenges and impacts of BEPS on global tax revenue. The chapter sheds light on the role of corporate tax havens and the specific industries that are most involved in these practices, critically examining the effectiveness of BEPS tools and the ethical dilemmas they present.

In Chapter Three, tax management strategies are dissected alongside ethical considerations. From tax-free income to tax deferral, the legal and moral pathways that individuals and corporations can safeguard their income from taxation are explored, emphasizing the significance of navigating tax planning with legal precision and ethical integrity and balancing tax avoidance strategies with societal responsibilities.

Chapter Four discusses corporate tax management, detailing the mechanisms of corporate tax, the benefits of strategic tax planning, and the impact of global tax systems on multinational enterprises. The chapter further explains the evolving nature of tax management in the face of globalization, digitalization, and regulatory changes, highlighting the necessity for adaptive strategies and compliance.

Mastering tax planning, as unveiled in Chapter Five, encapsulates strategies for maximizing savings for individuals and businesses. It presents a thorough tax planning process, from understanding essential taxes and their impacts to optimizing timing for tax planning actions. This chapter advocates for a strategic approach that minimizes tax liability and aligns with individual and business financial situations.

Chapter Six focuses on optimizing financial health through tax deductions, credits, and strategic planning. It explores the direct benefits of tax credits, the importance of tax deductions, and the role of tax exclusions in financial optimization. This chapter guides navigating federal and state tax credits, maximizing tax benefits, and planning for family-focused tax benefits.

Finally, Chapter Seven, grounded in the University of San Francisco case, brings to light the role of internal audit and tax compliance in ensuring operational integrity. It emphasizes the importance of effective tax risk management, detailing strategies for managing tax risks and highlighting the critical role of technology in tax administration.

The book is designed to help those seeking to understand the labyrinth of tax management in today's complex world. Inviting readers—be they students, professionals, or enthusiasts—to engage deeply with the principles of tax planning, the challenges of international taxation, and the ethical dimensions that underpin them all.

INTRODUCTION

"Strategic Tax Planning, Ethical Excellence, and International Taxation Challenges" is an authoritative guide that delves deep into the complexities of modern tax management, offering a comprehensive overview of strategic tax planning within corporate, nonprofit, and international taxation. This meticulously researched book is designed to equip readers with the knowledge and strategies to navigate the ever-evolving tax landscape, balancing profitability with compliance and leveraging legal tax-saving opportunities without compromising ethical standards.

From the foundational aspects of strategic tax management to the nuanced challenges of Base Erosion and Profit Shifting (BEPS) and the ethical considerations in tax planning, this book covers a broad spectrum of topics essential for today's professionals. It presents an in-depth analysis of corporate tax structures, key taxable events, and the intricacies of nonprofit taxation, alongside an exploration of the impact of global tax systems on multinational enterprises and the future trends in tax management.

Readers will gain insights into effective tax risk management strategies, the importance of internal audits, and the role of technology in enhancing tax administration and compliance. With a focus on optimizing financial health through tax deductions, credits, and strategic planning, the book offers valuable guidance on maximizing tax benefits while adhering to legal and ethical standards.

"Strategic Tax Planning, Ethical Excellence, And International Taxation Challenges" is an indispensable resource for students, tax professionals, corporate managers, and anyone interested in understanding the strategic and ethical dimensions of tax planning. Whether you want to deepen your knowledge of tax management or seek practical advice on navigating the complexities of international taxation, this book provides a wealth of information and insights to help you achieve financial success and integrity in your tax strategies.

In a world driven by commerce and governed by intricate financial systems, understanding taxation is not merely an option; it is a necessity. Welcome to "Strategic Tax Planning, Ethical Excellence, And International Taxation Challenges," a comprehensive exploration of the dynamic and complex world of taxation.

This book is a journey through the multifaceted realms of taxation, dissecting its core principles, ethical considerations, and international intricacies. As we venture further into its chapters, we will uncover the art of balancing profitability and compliance, the challenges of base erosion and profit shifting, the nuances of tax management strategies, and the implications of corporate tax planning. We will explore the strategies that enable individuals and businesses to maximize savings while maintaining ethical integrity. We will also delve into the pivotal role of internal audit and tax compliance in ensuring responsible financial practices.

CHAPTER ONE: STRATEGIC TAX MANAGEMENT: BALANCING PROFITABILITY AND COMPLIANCE

Summary of Key Points

1. Strategic Tax Planning: Strategic tax management involves aligning tax-related decisions with a company's financial goals to enhance profitability and competitiveness. Proper tax planning includes utilizing legal tax-saving opportunities and leveraging incentives to improve cash flow and profits.

2. Legal and Ethical Considerations: Effective tax management requires balancing legal tax optimization strategies with ethical standards. Companies must adhere to tax codes while maintaining transparent and responsible financial practices to avoid reputational risks.

3. Corporate Tax Structure and Key Taxable Events: Understanding the structure of corporate taxes, including federal and state obligations, and managing key taxable events like asset sales is essential for optimal tax positioning.

4. Nonprofit Taxation: Nonprofits must manage their tax-exempt status carefully, including handling Unrelated Business Income Tax (UBIT) to ensure financial sustainability.

5. Integration of Business Goals with Tax Strategies: Companies must synchronize their business objectives with tax strategies, considering both short-term and long-term goals, including assessing the balance

between tax-saving strategies and associated risks.

6. Tax Compliance and Risk Management: Adherence to tax laws is critical to avoid legal consequences. Companies should establish strong internal controls for accurate reporting and be prepared for audits to manage tax risks effectively.

Impact of Strategic Tax Management on Financial Performance

Strategic tax management involves carefully planned and executed tax-related decisions to optimize a company's financial performance. Effective tax management can significantly enhance a company's profitability and competitiveness by identifying tax-saving opportunities, reducing liabilities, and leveraging incentives. For example, efficient tax planning can reduce effective tax rates, improve cash flow, and increase after-tax profits. For instance, Apple Inc.'s tax strategies, such as utilizing offshore subsidiaries, are legal, although facing scrutiny, underscoring the significant impact of strategic tax decisions on a company's financial outcomes.

Balancing Legal and Ethical Considerations: Strategic tax management necessitates balancing legal tax optimization with ethical standards. Aggressive tax avoidance strategies, while legal, can pose reputational risks and legal challenges. Companies must adhere to complex tax codes and ethical norms, ensuring transparent and responsible financial practices, as exemplified by the LuxLeaks scandal, which highlighted ethical concerns in tax avoidance practices. Therefore, in-depth knowledge of tax laws is essential, including understanding different tax types and their impact on financial decisions and keeping abreast of regulatory changes. Strategies for minimizing tax liabilities should be legal and ethical, including tax credits, deductions, incentives, and efficient tax structures. Strategic tax management aligns financial goals with tax planning, optimizing performance while maintaining legal and ethical integrity.

Structure of Corporate Tax

It involves federal and potentially state corporate income taxes on a corporation's taxable income. In the U.S., the controversy around Amazon's minimal federal tax liability highlights the complexities of corporate tax structures.

Key Taxable Events for Businesses: Events like asset sales can trigger tax obligations. For instance, Google's acquisition of YouTube involved significant tax considerations, emphasizing the importance of managing these events for optimal tax positions.

Nonprofit Taxation: Nonprofits can obtain tax exemptions for income, donations, and property, enabling them to receive tax-deductible donations. Maintaining this status is crucial for financial sustainability, as seen in organizations like the American Red Cross. However, tax-exempt nonprofits may face UBIT on income from activities unrelated to their exempt purpose, necessitating careful management and reporting to ensure compliance.

In summary, mastering business taxation involves understanding corporate taxation basics, including the structure and key taxable events and the specifics of nonprofit taxation, such as tax-exempt status and UBIT. Real-world examples highlight the complexities and implications of these principles in the ever-evolving world of business taxation.

Principles of Strategic Tax Planning

Integration of Business Goals and Tax Strategies: Strategic tax planning requires synchronizing business objectives with appropriate tax strategies, focusing on immediate and future goals. Companies aiming for quick growth prioritize short-term tax benefits, such as tax credits, to boost cash flow. In contrast, those focused on long-term sustainability opt for tax plans that support reinvestment and research incentives. For example, Apple's 2018 repatriation of overseas profits, influenced by tax law changes, demonstrates a strategic alignment with its long-term goals and a keen adaptation to favorable tax conditions.

Balancing Risk and Reward: Tax planning involves weighing the benefits of tax-saving strategies against potential risks and compliance obligations. While aggressive tactics like tax shelters can provide short-term gains, they also carry risks of legal issues and damage to reputation. The key is to find a balance, employing tax strategies that are both beneficial and compliant. The downfall of Enron, partly due to its risky tax strategies, serves as a warning against overly aggressive approaches.

Tax Planning Lifecycle: From a company's inception, strategic tax planning is crucial, encompassing decisions on entity structure, accounting methods, and initial tax choices. For example, a startup opting for an LLC structure might benefit from pass-through taxation, aligning with early-stage goals of reducing tax burdens. Silicon Valley startups often consider tax-efficient structures for better valuations and venture capital attractiveness, mindful of the long-term tax implications of equity compensation and capitalization choices. Continuous tax planning is vital for businesses in operation and growth phases to maximize deductions, credits, and incentives within the evolving business context. A company expanding internationally, for instance, may structure its operations to leverage tax benefits across jurisdictions, aligning with global expansion goals. Starbucks' controversial tax strategies, involving profit shifting to low-tax areas, exemplify the challenges and scrutiny faced in ongoing operations.

Exit and Succession Planning: Tax planning for business transitions, whether through sales, mergers, or generational shifts, is essential for optimizing tax outcomes. Family businesses, for instance, may focus on estate planning to reduce estate taxes and ensure smooth generational transitions, preserving family wealth. The sale of a business requires careful planning to minimize capital gains taxes and maximize after-tax returns for shareholders.

In summary, strategic tax planning is a multifaceted process that involves aligning business objectives with tax strategies across different timeframes, managing risks and rewards, and adapting to changing business and regulatory landscapes. The lifecycle of tax planning, from a business's formation to its transition, demands continuous strategic adaptation, as illustrated by various real-world examples.

Understanding Tax Deductions and Credits

Ordinary and Necessary Expenses: Businesses can deduct 'ordinary' (common in the industry) and 'necessary' (helpful and appropriate for the business). For instance, a software company can deduct costs for computers and software licenses, which are essential for its operations. Similarly, a graphic design studio's investment in high-quality design software, a standard in the industry and crucial for their work, qualifies as a deductible expense.

Depreciation and Amortization: This allows businesses to deduct certain assets' costs gradually. Tangible assets are covered under depreciation, while intangible assets fall under amortization. For example, a manufacturing company can depreciate machinery over its useful life, while a tech firm might amortize the cost of a patent. A construction company might spread the cost of $500,000 worth of equipment over several years, reducing its taxable income annually through depreciation.

Tax Credits and Incentives: These may include Research and Development (R&D) and renewal energy credits. R&D credits incentivize businesses to invest in innovation, reducing their tax liability for qualified research expenses. A pharmaceutical company developing a new drug or a tech startup creating new software features could be eligible for these credits, encouraging technological advancement. Renewable energy credits, aimed at promoting clean energy, benefit businesses involved in renewable energy projects. For example, a solar energy company can earn credits for producing solar power, which can be traded or used to reduce tax liabilities. Tesla's use of renewable energy credits, both for its operations and as incentives for customers, highlights the role of these credits in supporting environmentally sustainable practices.

Understanding tax deductions and credits is essential for businesses to manage their tax liabilities effectively. Deductible expenses include routine and essential business costs, depreciation, and amortization of assets. Tax credits for R&D and renewable energy incentivize specific business activities, supporting innovation and sustainability. Cases like those of Tesla and various tech startups illustrate the strategic use of these tax benefits.

International Tax Considerations

It involves considerations of transfer pricing, tax treaties, and cross-border planning.

Arm's Length Principle: This principle ensures that transactions between related entities are priced as if between independent parties, aiming for fair and equitable taxation. Starbucks' case, involving accusations of artificially lowering taxable income through transfer pricing, underscores the importance of adhering to this principle. Similarly, a multinational tech company must price software licenses sold to its subsidiaries in line with market rates to comply.

Documentation and Compliance: Companies must maintain detailed records justifying their transfer pricing strategies. Alphabet Inc.'s settlement with France over tax disputes highlights the necessity of comprehensive documentation to support pricing decisions. A global manufacturing company, for example, would need to document its intercompany pricing strategy, including market analyses and comparable transactions, to demonstrate compliance.

Double Taxation Avoidance: Tax treaties help prevent the same income from being taxed in multiple countries. For example, the U.S.-Germany tax treaty provides guidelines for tax relief, preventing double taxation for businesses operating in both countries. A multinational corporation operating in the U.S. and the U.K. can similarly benefit from tax treaties, reducing the tax burden on income earned in both nations.

Structuring International Operations: Companies strategically structure their international operations for tax efficiency, selecting jurisdictions and legal structures to minimize global tax liabilities. Apple's use of Ireland and the 'Double Irish with a Dutch Sandwich' structure exemplifies strategic tax planning in international operations. A multinational retailer might establish a holding company in a tax-favorable jurisdiction to consolidate profits, optimizing its global tax position.

In summary, navigating international tax considerations involves understanding and applying principles like transfer pricing and the Arm's Length

Principle, backed by thorough documentation. Tax treaties are vital in avoiding double taxation, and strategic structuring of international operations is key to minimizing global tax liabilities. Examples from multinational companies highlight international tax management's complexities and strategic approaches."

Tax Compliance and Risk Management

The Criticality of Compliance: Legal Implications of Non-Compliance: Adherence to tax laws is essential for businesses to fulfill their legal obligations and avoid severe consequences like fines, penalties, or legal actions. In severe cases, non-compliance can even lead to business suspension. Tyco International's legal issues due to tax evasion schemes, resulting in substantial fines and reputation damage, underscore the serious legal risks of non-compliance.

Importance of Internal Controls and Audit Readiness: Establishing strong internal controls ensures accurate financial reporting and tax compliance. Companies must be prepared for audits by maintaining organized records and a comprehensive understanding of their tax positions. For example, an e-commerce company must implement controls to accurately document sales tax across different jurisdictions, ensuring compliance and simplifying the audit process.

Effective Tax Risk Management: Identifying and evaluating potential tax risks is a critical component of tax risk management. Factors like changes in tax laws, economic conditions, or business operations can introduce new tax risks. For instance, global supply chain disruptions could affect transfer pricing arrangements, increasing tax risks. The "Paradise Papers" leak, revealing complex offshore structures to reduce tax liabilities, highlighted the reputational risks of aggressive tax planning.

Mitigating Tax Risks: Companies use various strategies to minimize tax risks, such as engaging in prudent tax planning, seeking legal opinions, and adopting conservative tax positions. To ensure compliance, a multinational corporation might seek a tax authority ruling or legal opinion for a complex transaction. Proactive tax planning, as seen in a pharmaceutical company optimizing tax incentives for research and development, mitigates tax risks and boosts industry competitiveness.

In summary, tax compliance is vital for legal adherence and financial stability, while managing tax risks involves assessing challenges and implementing strategies to mitigate them. Examples from the corporate world illustrate the consequences of non-compliance and the importance of effective risk management in the complex tax environment.

Ethical and Social Responsibility in Taxation

CSR and Ethical Tax Practices: As part of Corporate Social Responsibility (CSR), transparent tax reporting is crucial. It involves disclosing tax information to stakeholders, promoting accountability, and building trust. Starbucks, for instance, increased transparency post-criticism by publishing annual tax reports, offering stakeholders insights into its tax contributions and policies. A technology company might disclose its effective tax rate and incentive details to enhance stakeholder trust.

Distinguishing Ethical Tax Planning from Evasion: It is important to differentiate between legal tax avoidance and illegal tax evasion. Tax avoidance uses legal means to minimize liabilities, while evasion involves unlawful practices. Google's defense of its tax strategies highlights this distinction. The Panama Papers scandal, revealing offshore tax evasion, exemplifies unethical tax behavior's legal and reputational risks.

Ethical and Social Considerations in Taxation: Ethical tax practices entail fair and responsible contributions to the communities where businesses operate, including adhering to laws and balancing the interests of various stakeholders. Ethical practices impact all stakeholders and contribute to long-term business sustainability and reputation. Engaging constructively with tax authorities and ensuring compliance is part of ethical behavior. For instance, a multinational pharmaceutical company dedicated to ethical taxation transparently discloses its tax policies in its annual CSR report. It engages in lawful tax planning and emphasizes its contribution to community development.

In summary, ethical and socially responsible taxation involves transparency, fair contribution, and a conscientious approach to tax planning and evasion. Businesses committed to ethical practices enhance their corporate image and foster public trust.

Technology and Tax Management

Harnessing Technology for Tax Efficiency: Technology integration in tax management, through tools like QuickBooks and TurboTax, streamlines processes, improves accuracy and ensures compliance. These solutions automate routine tasks, allowing professionals to focus on strategic tax management. A multinational corporation might use such software for global financial data consolidation, transfer pricing adjustments, and compliance in various jurisdictions.

Data Analytics in Strategic Tax Planning: Data analytics is pivotal in tax planning, enabling businesses to analyze large datasets, identify patterns, and make strategic decisions. Predictive analytics can forecast financial trends, aiding in tax liability estimation and optimization strategies. For instance, a retail company could use analytics to understand customer behaviors and optimize sales tax strategies.

Advancements in Tax Management Technology: Blockchain technology ensures secure, transparent transactions, while AI and machine learning algorithms predict risks and optimize tax strategies. Cloud-based solutions offer flexibility and collaboration, which are essential for modern tax management. For instance, an international accounting firm employs advanced technology, including blockchain for secure transactions, AI for data analysis, and cloud-based platforms for collaboration, enhancing client services and ensuring efficient tax management.

In summary, leveraging technology in tax management is essential for efficiency, accuracy, and compliance. Automation, data analytics, and technological advancements enable organizations to navigate the complex tax landscape effectively, making informed decisions for strategic financial management.

Case Studies and Best Practices in Tax Management

Apple Inc. in the Technology Sector: Apple exemplifies strategic international tax planning by optimizing its global tax position through favorable tax jurisdictions and legal strategies. This approach highlights the importance of strategic tax planning for multinational corporations.

Procter & Gamble (P&G) in Consumer Goods: P&G aligns its tax strategy with its focus on innovation, utilizing tax incentives for research and development to maximize benefits from tax credits and deductions.

JPMorgan Chase in Financial Services: JPMorgan Chase adeptly manages its tax liabilities by optimizing its corporate structure, demonstrating how companies in the financial sector can navigate complex tax regulations to leverage deductions and credits.

Key Lessons and Strategies

1. Strategic Alignment: Successful tax management aligns with a company's overall business strategy, whether focusing on global expansion, innovation, or operational efficiency.
2. Adaptability: Businesses must stay agile, adapting to evolving tax laws and regulations to maintain compliance and capitalize on new opportunities.
3. Risk Assessment: Conducting thorough risk assessments enables proactive identification and management of potential tax challenges.
4. Transparency and Communication: Clear reporting and communication about tax strategies and compliance enhance a company's reputation and stakeholder trust.
5. Technology Integration: Utilizing technology in tax management, such as automation and analytics, streamlines processes and supports informed decision-making.

Illustrative Scenario: ABC Pharma, a multinational pharmaceutical company, exemplifies effective tax management. By aligning its tax strategy with innovation goals, it qualifies for research tax credits. The company structures its international operations to leverage tax treaties and optimize transfer pricing, mitigating double taxation risks. ABC Pharma's transparency in tax strategies within annual reports and CSR disclosures builds stakeholder trust.

The above case studies demonstrate the significance of strategic alignment, regulatory adaptability, risk assessment, transparency, and technology integration in optimizing tax positions and ensuring financial sustainability.

Future Trends in Tax Management

Shifting Regulatory Landscape: Digital transaction taxation challenges tax authorities, demanding special regulations. Global regulators are focusing on taxing digital transactions and services. For example, the European Union's Digital Services Tax proposal targets large tech companies, aiming to adapt tax policies to the digital economy. Tax authorities are adopting technologies like AI and blockchain for more efficient, transparent, and compliant processes. Equally, governments are increasingly implementing green taxes, like carbon taxes, to promote eco-friendly business practices. These taxes align corporate activities with global climate change initiatives.

Global Taxation Framework: The push for a unified global taxation system, led by organizations like the OECD, addresses issues like profit shifting and aims to establish a global minimum corporate tax rate. As digital taxation and environmental tax policies evolve, a multinational corporation adjusts its tax strategy to align with these changes. The company integrates green policies into its operations and invests in advanced technologies for effective tax management, positioning itself to navigate the future taxation landscape. Digital taxation, environmental considerations, and global regulatory cooperation will shape the future of tax management. Businesses must adapt to these changes, embrace technology, and engage constructively with global tax initiatives to successfully navigate the dynamic world of taxation.

Anticipated Impacts and Strategies

1. Compliance Challenges: Businesses operating must adapt to legislative changes and engage proactively with tax authorities.
2. Embracing Technology: Investing in digital capabilities will be crucial for efficient and compliant tax management in a rapidly evolving landscape.

Review Questions

1. How does strategic tax planning contribute to a company's profitability and competitiveness?
2. What are the key considerations in balancing legal tax optimization with ethical standards?
3. What is the importance of understanding corporate tax structure and key taxable events in business?
4. How do nonprofits manage their tax-exempt status and handle UBIT?
5. How can businesses align their tax strategies with their business goals?
6. Why are tax compliance and risk management critical for businesses, and what practices support this?

Discussion Points

1. Debate the Ethical Implications: Discuss the ethical implications of aggressive tax avoidance strategies used by large corporations and their impact on societal perception.
2. Evolving Tax Landscape: Consider businesses' challenges in adapting to rapidly changing tax laws, especially in the digital economy, and discuss strategies for staying compliant.
3. Technology in Tax Management: Explore the role of technology in enhancing tax management efficiency and compliance and discuss future trends in tax technology.

CHAPTER TWO: BASE EROSION AND PROFIT SHIFTING (BEPS) IN INTERNATIONAL TAXATION

Summary of Key Points

1. Introduction to BEPS: BEPS is a complex issue in international taxation where multinational corporations use strategies to shift profits from higher-tax to lower-tax jurisdictions, eroding the tax base of higher-tax countries.

2. BEPS Impact: BEPS practices reduce tax revenue for higher-tax jurisdictions and disproportionately affect developing nations that rely on corporate income tax.

3. Role of Corporate Tax Havens: Corporate tax havens significantly facilitate BEPS by offering profit-shifting tools and mechanisms to avoid taxes.

4. Industries Involved: Industries with valuable intellectual property (I.P.) assets, like Technology and Life Sciences, are often engaged in BEPS activities due to I.P. mobility.

5. Historical Association with U.S. Multinationals: BEPS activities have historically been associated with U.S. multinationals, driven by the worldwide taxation approach.

6. Effectiveness of BEPS Tools: The effectiveness of BEPS tools relies on corporate tax havens having a network of bilateral tax treaties that accept these tools.

Base Erosion and Profit Shifting (BEPS)

Base Erosion and Profit Shifting (BEPS) is a complex international taxation issue involving multinational corporations employing strategies to relocate profits from higher-tax jurisdictions to lower-tax or even tax-free locations with minimal economic activity. This practice erodes the tax base of the higher-tax jurisdictions, as companies make deductible payments, such as interest or royalties, to shift their profits. In essence, the income or profit on which taxes are levied is moved to another country or tax haven, resulting in reduced tax revenue for the originating country and fiscal challenges. The Organization for Economic Cooperation and Development (OECD) defines BEPS strategies as exploiting gaps and mismatches in tax rules. While some of these tactics may be illegal, many are not, creating concerns about the fairness and integrity of tax systems. BEPS activities disproportionately affect developing nations that heavily rely on corporate income tax, exacerbating the issue.

Corporate tax havens play a significant role in facilitating BEPS by offering tools to shift profits to these havens and additional mechanisms to avoid paying taxes within them. This results in substantial revenue losses for nations, estimated at $100-240 billion annually, which accounts for 4-10 percent of the total global corporate income tax collection. Notably, American technology and life science multinationals are often associated with the widespread use of BEPS tools.

The primary industries involved in BEPS activities are those with significant intellectual property (I.P.) assets, such as Technology (e.g., Apple, Google, Microsoft, Oracle) and Life Sciences (e.g., Allergan, Medtronic, Pfizer, Merck & Co). I.P., which includes patents, trademarks, and copyrights, is highly mobile and can be relocated to low-tax jurisdictions without substantial costs, making it attractive for multinational tax planning. Multinationals often create separate companies in tax havens to hold and license I.P. rights, allowing them to shift profits efficiently. Another standard BEPS method involves intra-group debts, which are debts within a corporate group. These debts are easy to create and manipulate, often requiring no asset movement or significant operational changes. Intra-group debts are not typically recognized under accounting standards and do not affect the consolidated financial statements of multinational companies.

BEPS activities have historically been associated with U.S. multinationals, partly due to the U.S. tax system, which operated under a "worldwide" taxation approach before the Tax Cuts and Jobs Act of 2017 (TCJA). Under this system, U.S. multinationals had incentives to shift profits to lower-tax jurisdictions. U.S. multinationals also extensively use tax havens, with a significant share of global profits shifted to these jurisdictions. In summary, BEPS is a complex issue involving multinational tax planning strategies that shift profits to lower-tax locations, eroding the tax base of higher-tax jurisdictions. This practice has significant implications for tax revenue, especially in developing countries, and is associated with industries with valuable intellectual property assets. U.S. multinationals have been prominent in BEPS activities, although recent tax reforms have aimed to address some of these issues.

In June 2018, research highlighted Ireland as the world's largest hub for Base Erosion and Profit Shifting (BEPS). It is worth noting that Ireland surpasses the entire Caribbean tax haven BEPS system, excluding Bermuda. The top 10 global tax havens align closely with the most significant global BEPS hubs, as illustrated in the Zucman-Tørsløv-Wier table below:

Research from September 2018, based on repatriation tax data from the TCJA, found that approximately half of the foreign profits of U.S. multinationals were booked in tax haven affiliates, primarily in Ireland (18%), Switzerland, Bermuda, and Caribbean tax havens (8%-9% each). This solidified Ireland's position as the top tax haven, with U.S. firms booking more profits in Ireland than in China, Japan, Germany, France, and Mexico combined, despite its low tax rate of 5.7%.

The effectiveness of BEPS tools relies on corporate tax havens having a network of bilateral tax treaties that accept these tools, allowing profits to be shifted there. Modern corporate tax havens, the central hubs for BEPS, maintain extensive networks of these treaties, with the U.K. leading with over 122 and the Netherlands following with over 100. These tax havens work diligently to adhere to OECD standards to avoid being blocked, as it is a significant event.

A pivotal academic study in July 2017, referred to as "Conduit and Sink OFCs," revealed that the pressure to maintain OECD compliance had divided corporate-focused tax havens into two categories: Sink OFCs, which act as the final destination for BEPS flows, and Conduit OFCs, which serve as intermediaries for flows from higher-tax locations to Sink OFCs. Notably, the top five Conduit OFCs— Ireland, the Netherlands, the United Kingdom, Singapore, and Switzerland— all ranked in the top ten of the 2018 Global Innovation Property Centre (GIPC) I.P. Index.

Once profits are shifted to corporate tax havens or Conduit OFCs, additional tools are employed to avoid paying the headline tax rates in those havens. Some of these tools are OECD-compliant, such as patent boxes and Capital Allowances for Intangible Assets (CAIA), while others have been proscribed by the OECD, like the Double Irish and Dutch Double-Dipping. Some tools, such as to attract Malt arrangement, have yet to attract OECD attention. BEPS hubs or Conduit OFCs need extensive bilateral tax treaties to ensure higher-tax locations accept their BEPS tools. To maintain secrecy and avoid full disclosure, they utilize financial secrecy laws and often do not require multinational corporations to file public accounts or country-by-country reporting.

These BEPS hubs vehemently deny being corporate tax havens and argue that using intellectual property (I.P.) is a means of economic development rather than tax avoidance. They often refer to themselves as "knowledge economies." Understanding that tax evasion and aggressive tax planning do not primarily stem from the headline tax rate but result from schemes designed to facilitate profit shifting is essential.

Table 1: Missing Profits of Nations – Shifted Profits (2015)

Accounting Tools and Tax Legislation

The intricate accounting tools and comprehensive tax legislation required for corporate tax havens to meet OECD compliance as BEPS hubs involve two critical elements: advanced international tax-law professional services firms and close coordination with the State. These specialized firms navigate the complexities of international tax law while governments incorporate BEPS tools into their statutory legislation. Tax investigators often call These jurisdictions " captured states, " indicating their alignment with tax avoidance practices. Most prominent BEPS hubs typically started as established financial centers with pre-existing skills and state support for tax avoidance tools.

It is worth noting that the existence and discussion of BEPS tools have been known in Washington for decades. For instance, when the EU-OECD pressured Ireland to close its double Irish BEPS tool in January 2015, existing users like Google and Facebook received a five-year extension until 2020. Even before 2015, Ireland had already replaced the double Irish with two new BEPS tools: the single malt (utilized by Microsoft and Allergan) and capital allowances for intangible assets (known as the "Green Jersey," used by Apple in Q1 2015). Notably, none of the ESPS tools have been proscribed to be by the OECD, and disputes between higher-tax jurisdictions and tax havens are infrequent.

Tax experts present a nuanced perspective, suggesting that Washington implicitly accepted that U.S. multinationals could employ BEPS tools on non-U.S. earnings to offset the historically high U.S. 35 percent corporate tax rate under the "worldwide" corporate tax system. Some experts, including James R. Hines Jr., a leading tax haven researcher, argue that U.S. multinationals' use of BEPS tools and corporate tax havens has increased long-term tax receipts for the U.S. Treasury, albeit at the expense of other higher-tax jurisdictions. Various studies demonstrate that lower foreign tax rates result in more minor foreign tax credits and ultimately lead to higher U.S. tax collections. The 1994 Hines-Rice paper was the first to introduce the term "profit shifting" and concluded that low foreign tax rates from tax havens ultimately enhance U.S. tax collections. For instance, the Tax Cuts and Jobs Act of 2017 imposed a 15.5 percent tax on untaxed offshore cash reserves accumulated by U.S.

multinationals using BEPS tools from 2004 to 2017. Had these multinationals paid their total foreign taxes, their foreign tax credits would have largely nullified any U.S. tax liability.

The U.S. was among the major developed nations that did not sign the 2016 OECD initiative to curb BEPS tools. The G20 Los Cabos Summit 2012 tasked the OECD with developing a BEPS Action Plan, which was approved at the 2013 G-20 St. Petersburg summit. This project aimed to prevent profit shifting from higher- to lower-tax jurisdictions. The OECD BEPS Multilateral Instrument, consisting of 15 Actions designed for domestic implementation and bilateral tax treaties, was agreed upon at the 2015 G20 Antalya summit. It was adopted in November 2016 and has since been signed by over 78 jurisdictions, coming into force in July 2018. Some tax havens opted out of specific Actions, including Action 12 (Disclosure of aggressive tax planning), due to corporate opposition. Global legal firm Baker McKenzie represented a coalition of 24 multinational U.S. software firms, including Microsoft, lobbying against the OECD MLI proposals in 2017, expressing concerns about the potential impact on taxation and investment.

While the TCJA of 2017 introduced anti-BEPS tool regimes, it also included BEPS tools like the FDII-tax regime. This shift from a "worldwide" to a "territorial" tax system raised expectations that U.S. multinationals would no longer need foreign BEPS tools. However, by mid-2018, they had not repatriated these tools, and evidence suggested an increased reliance on corporate tax havens. In May 2018, it became evident that the TCJA had technical issues that incentivized actions like doubling office space in Ireland by companies like Google and executing Apple's Irish BEPS tool by Microsoft. Some debates revolve around whether these issues are drafting mistakes or concessions to reduce effective corporate tax rates.

In February 2019, Brad Setser from the Council on Foreign Relations highlighted concerns regarding the TCJA's effectiveness in curtailing U.S. corporate use of significant tax havens such as Ireland, the Netherlands, and Singapore. Following his New York Times article, Setser expressed doubt about the effectiveness of both the OECD's base erosion and profit shifting (BEPS) efforts and the U.S. Tax Cuts and Jobs Act (TCJA) in curbing major U.S.

companies' ability to significantly reduce their tax burden by shifting profits offshore. Companies have been paying minimal taxes (between 0–3 percent) on offshore profits, and even after accounting for the GILTI 10.5 percent tax rate, which deducts foreign taxes paid and tangible assets abroad, they still manage to lower their overall tax liability. Setser noted that the scale of profit shifting has become so significant that it distorts Irish economic data and U.S. GDP figures. He suggested that the TCJA's failure to address this issue might necessitate further reforms in the future.

On January 29, 2019, the OECD introduced a policy note outlining new proposals by multinational corporations to combat BEPS activities, dubbed "BEPS 2.0." These proposals garnered support from major economies, including the U.S., China, Brazil, and India. Irish media highlighted a potential threat to Ireland, the world's largest BEPS hub, as the OECD considered shifting to a global taxation system based on where products are consumed or used rather than where intellectual property (I.P.) is located. This shift in approach could disadvantage smaller countries like Ireland, which have a limited number of consumers or users. PwC's Head of Tax in Ireland noted that this change would primarily benefit larger countries with more significant consumer bases.

OECD's Two Pillar Solution

As of October 8, 2021, the OECD has introduced a Two-Pillar Solution to address tax challenges arising from digitalization:

Pillar One targets multinational enterprises (MNEs) with global turnover exceeding 20 billion euros and profitability over 10 percent, possibly reducing the turnover threshold to 10 billion euros. Extractives and regulated financial services are excluded. The determination of the tax base relies on financial accounting income with a few adjustments, and losses can be carried forward. Double taxation of profit allocated to market jurisdictions is relieved using the exemption or credit method. The entity responsible for the tax liability will be selected from those earning residual profit. The relevant review of this solution begins seven years after its implementation and should conclude in no more than one year.

The Pillar Two framework comprises two interconnected sets of domestic rules, collectively referred to as the Global Anti-base Erosion Rules (GloBE rules):

1. Income Inclusion Rule (IIR): This rule mandates a parent entity to pay additional taxes on the low-taxed income its constituent entity generates.
2. Undertaxed Payment Rule (UTPR): The UTPR denies deductions or requires an equivalent adjustment when the low-taxed income of a constituent entity is not subjected to tax under the IIR.

The GloBE rules apply to Multinational Enterprises (MNEs) meeting or exceeding the 750 million euros threshold established by BEPS Action 13 (country-by-country reporting). Countries can apply the IIR to MNEs headquartered within their jurisdiction, even if they fall below the threshold. However, entities such as government bodies, international organizations, non-profit organizations, pension funds, investment funds, or any holding vehicles utilized by these entities are exempt from the GloBE rules, provided they serve as the Ultimate Parent Entities (UPE) of an MNE Group.

In addition to these domestic rules, a treaty-based provision is known as the Subject-To-Tax Rule (STTR). The STTR allows source jurisdictions to impose limited source taxation on specific related party payments if they are subject to tax below a specified minimum rate. Any tax collected under the STTR can be credited as a covered tax under the GloBE rules.

In 2013, the OECD, in collaboration with the G20, initiated the BEPS Project to equip governments with tools to combat tax avoidance by international companies. This project encompasses 15 Actions, offering recommendations to governments to deter profit shifting. One such recommendation involves avoiding direct taxation on digital products while the project also promotes enhanced cooperation and information sharing among countries. The G20, in partnership with the OECD, actively participates in the BEPS Project. In 2015, the G20 endorsed transfer pricing recommendations designed to guide governments on allocating multinational company profits equitably among individual countries. Additionally, the G20 has been instrumental in formulating a global tax framework. In 2021, the G20 approved a framework for international tax reform, guiding the implementation of a global minimum tax.

E.U.'s Anti-Tax Avoidance Directive (ATAD)

In 2016, the European Union (E.U.) adopted the Anti-Tax Avoidance Directive (ATAD), aligning with the BEPS project's recommendations. The ATAD seeks to implement these recommendations effectively. In 2017, the E.U. introduced mandatory disclosure rules for tax planning intermediaries, obliging them to report information to tax authorities to aid in identifying and addressing BEPS issues. The E.U. is also actively contributing to developing an international tax framework to establish a global minimum tax rate for multinational companies. The E.U. has signed multiple international tax treaties and has been working to implement them to combat BEPS. Moreover, the E.U. has been involved in discussions concerning the development of the Common Consolidated Corporate Tax Base (CCCTB), which aims to reduce opportunities for tax planning.

The United Nations (U.N.), through the Committee of Experts on International Cooperation in Tax Matters, has been engaged in combating BEPS. The committee has played a role in developing the U.N. Model Tax Convention, guiding governments on taxation rights and preventing double taxation. Furthermore, the U.N. has contributed to developing the Automatic Exchange of Information (AEOI) standard, which furnishes tax authorities with additional information about multinational companies, aiding in identifying BEPS issues.

Effective Tax Management for Enhanced Competitiveness

Companies should engage in strategic tax management practices to ensure business competitiveness, periodically reassess their tax strategies, and seek tax-related opportunities. Achieving corporate objectives depends on various factors, and strategic tax management involves minimizing the tax impact by identifying opportunities and conducting regular analyses. While the Brazilian tax system is often associated with heavy taxation, the complexity of tax laws and the time-consuming tax calculation process pose significant challenges to the business environment. Despite efforts to simplify tax processes in the country, these complexities persist. However, within this intricate landscape, there are opportunities for companies to position themselves more strategically and profitably with the proper guidance.

Tax Planning

Tax planning is a fundamental strategy for reducing business costs. This process includes choosing an appropriate taxation regime, such as the Simplified Taxation System, Taxable Income, or Presumed Profit. The choice of regime should align with the business's reality and objectives. Selecting the wrong path can lead to financial inefficiencies and increased costs, ultimately affecting the company's competitiveness. Tax planning is not a one-time effort but an ongoing process, especially during changes in business direction and legislative developments relevant to specific industries. It is crucial to involve different sectors within a company, as tax planning requires a collaborative approach to achieve results that best serve the company's needs.

Tax Benefits

Tax benefits are mechanisms designed to reduce or eliminate federal, State, and local tax burdens, promoting industry or regional development. These benefits can manifest as tax exemptions, reductions in the tax base, presumed tax credits, zero-rated taxes, tax deferrals, and more. Evaluating tax benefits is a company-specific endeavor, considering factors such as business segment, size, location, and tax regime. To leverage tax benefits effectively, companies must conduct technical studies, assess the feasibility of tax treatment, understand the conditions for benefit entitlement, navigate the requisite procedures at the appropriate levels, and monitor the duration and renewal deadlines associated with these benefits. Each company's unique circumstances should guide the utilization of tax benefits for maximum competitiveness.

Leveraging Tax Benefits: Under tax laws, companies can support preapproved social, cultural, and sports projects by allocating a portion of their existing tax obligations to these causes, incurring no additional costs. From an Institutional Marketing perspective, this offers a compelling opportunity to strengthen a brand's image as a catalyst for social progress.

Tax Review

Tax review is a strategic initiative to enhance a company's tax position. This process involves mapping all tax-related choices and decisions made by the business over the past five years.

Effective Tax Management Strategies

Tax complexity is a global reality, necessitating compliance with existing regulations. However, companies can enhance their tax process management to reduce costs, enhance security, and increase efficiency. Leveraging technology and integrated information systems is crucial to generating high-quality data, minimizing rework, and mitigating the risk of fines, penalties, and audits. Tax season can be a stressful period for both individuals and businesses. However, with strategic tax management, it is possible to transform the annual burden into an opportunity for significant tax savings. Adopting the right strategies and making informed decisions can effectively reduce your tax liability. Seven powerful ways to maximize tax savings through strategic tax management are discussed below.

Utilize Tax-Advantaged Accounts: One of the most effective ways to save on taxes is by leveraging tax-advantaged accounts, such as individual retirement accounts (IRAs) and 401(k) plans. These accounts offer immediate tax benefits through deductions or deferrals for contributions. Additionally, the growth of these contributions is tax-free until withdrawal, potentially resulting in substantial long-term tax savings.

Leverage Tax Deductions and Credits: Familiarize yourself with the various tax deductions and credits available. Deductions lower your taxable income, while credits directly reduce your tax liability. Standard deductions include mortgage interest, student loan interest, and medical expenses, while tax credits like the Child Tax Credit and the Earned Income Tax Credit can yield significant savings. Identifying and claiming these deductions and credits can significantly reduce your tax bill.

Implement Tax-Loss Harvesting: Tax-loss harvesting is a strategy commonly used by investors. It involves selling investments that have experienced losses to offset capital gains. By realizing these losses, you can reduce your taxable income and potentially offset taxes on your gains. Proper execution of tax-loss harvesting while adhering to rules and limitations can lead to substantial tax savings.

Strategically Plan Charitable Contributions: Charitable donations not only support worthy causes annual tax savings. Plan your charitable contributions strategically by donating appreciated assets such as stocks or real estate. This allows you to avoid paying capital gains taxes on the appreciation while benefiting from a deduction based on the donation's fair market value.

Maximize Retirement Contributions: Retribution to retirement accounts secures your financial future and provides immediate tax advantages. Make the most of your employer-sponsored retirement plans like 401(k)s contributions to benefit from employer matches and tax deductions. If eligible, consider contributing to Health Savings Accounts (HSAs), which offer triple tax advantages: tax-deductible contributions, tax-free growth, and tax-free withdrawals for qualified medical expenses.

Optimize Business Structure: Efficiently structuring your business can result in significant tax savings. Depending on your circumstances, options such as incorporation, partnership formation, or establishing a limited liability company (LLC) can provide various tax benefits. Consult with an expert to determine the optimal structure for your business and leverage potential deductions and credits.

Stay Informed about Tax Law Changes: Tax laws and regulations are subject to change, making it essential to stay informed for maximum tax savings. Keep abreast of updates and consult a tax advisor to ensure you utilize all available deductions, credits, and strategies. By staying proactive and adapting your tax planning accordingly, you can stay ahead of changes and optimize your tax savings.

To maximize tax savings, organizations need expert guidance for a profound understanding of the jurisdiction's tax laws. At the same time, the government should be committed to helping individuals and businesses thrive financially.

Review Questions

1. What is Base Erosion and Profit Shifting (BEPS) in international taxation, and why is it a significant issue?
2. How do corporate tax havens facilitate BEPS activities, and what role do they play in profit shifting?
3. Why are industries with intellectual property (I.P.) assets often involved in BEPS activities?
4. What was the historical association between BEPS activities and U.S. multinationals, and how did tax reforms address this?
5. What factors contribute to the effectiveness of BEPS tools, and why do corporate tax havens maintain extensive networks of tax treaties?
6. What are the potential consequences of the OECD's "BEPS 2.0" proposals for multinational corporations and smaller countries like Ireland?

Discussion Points

1. Discuss the ethical considerations surrounding BEPS activities and their impact on developing nations.
2. Debate the effectiveness of tax reforms in curbing BEPS activities, particularly in the context of U.S. multinationals.
3. Explore the potential implications of a global taxation system based on where products are consumed rather than where intellectual property is

located, as proposed by the OECD's "BEPS 2.0."

CHAPTER THREE: TAX MANAGEMENT STRATEGIES AND ETHICAL CONSIDERATIONS

Summary of Key Points

1. Tax-Free Income:

- Tax-free income allows withdrawals from federally qualified accounts in retirement without triggering ordinary income tax.
- Municipal bonds and Roth IRAs are examples of sources of tax-free income.
- Cash-value life insurance policies can generate tax-free earnings if IRS rules are followed.

2. Tax Deferral:

- Tax deferral is a strategy that postpones tax payments on investment growth until funds are withdrawn.
- It can be advantageous for individuals in higher tax brackets during their working years and lower brackets in retirement.
- Available through employer-sponsored qualified plans, IRAs, and annuities.

3. Navigating Tax Planning with Legal Precision and Ethical Integrity:

- Legal compliance and ethical considerations are vital in tax planning.
- Staying informed and accurate and making strategic decisions are essential in legal compliance.
- Transparency, fairness, and social responsibility are critical ethical considerations.

4. Tax Avoidance:

- Tax avoidance involves legally minimizing tax liabilities through strategies like capital investment relief, tax-exempt ISAs, and pension contributions.
- Ethical issues arise when tax liabilities are aggressively avoided through schemes not intended or authorized by the state.

5. Exploring Tax Management Strategies and Minimizing Tax Liability:

- Strategies to minimize tax liability include increasing retirement contributions, profiting from investment losses, contributing to traditional plans, and donating to charity.
- Consultation with a tax professional is recommended for personalized guidance.

6. Strategies to Safeguard Your Income from Taxation: Strategies include investing in municipal bonds, favoring long-term capital gains, starting a business, maximizing retirement contributions, utilizing HSAs, and claiming tax credits.

Effective Tax Management and Ethical Considerations – The US Case

Taxes are an inevitable part of our lives, but they need not be a heavy burden. Various techniques and methods exist for managing and preparing taxes that can help reduce your tax liability and optimize deductions and credits in the present and future. Tax accountants and tax planners can assist in reducing your tax burden as much as is legally possible. Considering the long-term tax implications of your investment and retirement savings decisions is essential. By doing so, you can position yourself to exercise significant tax control during retirement, precisely when it may be needed most.

Tax-Free Income

Tax-free income refers to the ability to withdraw funds from federally qualified accounts in retirement without triggering ordinary income tax. This offers flexibility in navigating the ever-changing tax policies of federal, state, and local authorities and provides a secure source of funds for unexpected expenses without complicating your tax filings. The IRS generally prefers all accounts to become taxable eventually. There are limited options to generate tax-free earnings. For instance, investors can consider municipal bonds, whose dividends are federally tax-free. Some municipalities even offer bonds exempt from both state and federal taxes. However, it is essential to note that this bond interest does appear on your tax forms and can impact the portion of Social Security subject to taxation.

Another avenue for tax-free income is distributions from Roth IRAs, which provide greater investment flexibility. Accessing tax-free income through Roth IRAs may require careful planning to build a substantial source of such income, and contributions to Roth IRAs may not be allowed for individuals above specific Modified Adjusted Gross Income (MAGI) limits.

A third, often overlooked, approach to generating tax-free earnings involves using cash-value life insurance policies. Many permanent life insurance policies accumulate accessible cash value over time through indexing, dividends, or specified interest rates. This growth can be accessed without incurring taxes, provided distributions adhere to basic IRS rules for tax-free life insurance distributions.

Tax Deferral

Tax deferral is a tax status applicable to certain account types and investment products. When investments grow in a tax-deferred account, investors are not required to pay annual capital gains taxes on that growth. Instead, taxes are deferred until the funds are withdrawn, allowing for compounding growth without annual tax liabilities. The tax deferral strategy can be advantageous in a financial plan by allowing taxes to accumulate while the investor is typically in a higher tax bracket during their working years. When the investor eventually withdraws and utilizes the funds in retirement, the expectation is to be in a lower tax bracket, resulting in overall tax savings. Tax deferral is available through various employer-sponsored qualified plans (such as 401(k)s and 403(b)s), IRAs, and non-qualified variable and fixed annuities.

Navigating Tax Planning with Legal Precision and Ethical Integrity

Meeting legal requirements in tax planning is as important as upholding the highest ethical standards. It ensures that our financial decisions, optimized for benefits, align with a broader sense of responsibility and integrity. Taxation laws are extensive and diverse, making legal compliance fundamental in financial planning. However, the ethical perspective from which the laws are approached is equally crucial. While the legal framework dictates what is permissible, ethics guide us in determining what is morally right.

Understanding the Legal Landscape involves:

Legal compliance in tax planning entails more than just adherence to rules; it necessitates a deep understanding of the tax code and its frequent changes. This includes:

1. Staying Informed: Keeping abreast of the latest tax laws and regulations

is imperative.

2. Accuracy and Honesty: Ensuring all information provided in tax filings is accurate and complete.
3. Strategic Decisions: Employing legal tax-saving strategies such as retirement contributions, charitable donations, and investment losses.

Ethical Considerations in Tax Planning involves: Ethical tax planning extends beyond mere legal compliance; it involves making decisions that reflect our values. This encompasses:

1. Transparency: Being open about financial practices and avoiding deception in any form.
2. Fairness: Considering the spirit of the law, not just its letter, and avoiding aggressive tax avoidance schemes.
3. Social Responsibility: Acknowledging that taxes contribute to societal welfare and approaching taxation with a sense of civic duty.

The balance between legal compliance and ethical responsibility can be delicate. For instance, while tax avoidance (minimizing tax within the law) is legal, it may only sometimes align with everyone's ethical standards. In contrast, tax evasion (illegally avoiding tax) is unethical and illegal. Effective tax planning involves making well-informed decisions that account for legal and ethical implications. This entails:

1. Consulting with Professionals: Collaborating with knowledgeable tax professionals who can guide you on complex tax matters.
2. Regular Reviews: Review tax strategies to ensure they align with current laws and ethical standards.
3. Personal Values: Reflecting on personal or business values to ensure tax strategies are consistent with these principles.

Tax planning is not merely a financial task but reflects our fiscal responsibility approach.

Tax Avoidance

Paying taxes to fund public policy initiatives and investments is a central necessity in most societies, and most individuals meet these expectations. However, while some criminally evade their tax responsibilities or fraudulently deceive the government, others exhibit varying levels of non-compliance, prompting ethical considerations about minimizing tax payments. However, there are legal and approved methods of "avoiding" tax liabilities for individuals and businesses. Reducing your tax bill through effective planning is legal, ethical, and, in some forms, encouraged by government-authorized schemes. For example, claiming tax relief on capital investment, saving in a tax-exempt ISA, or contributing to a pension scheme are all legitimate forms of tax planning. The critical point in tax avoidance is obtaining tax relief in ways that align with the government's intentions. However, ethical issues arise when tax liabilities are aggressively avoided through creative schemes not intended or authorized by the state but still adhering to the letter of the law. This is commonly referred to as "tax avoidance." While formally legal, it is highly questionable, potentially harmful, and often unethical.

Exploring Tax Management Strategies and Minimizing Tax Liability

Tax games

Recent revelations, such as the Paradise Papers, have again cast a spotlight on the practice of tax avoidance and its ethical considerations. Similar scandals, such as the Panama Papers in 2016 and the Swiss/HSBC leaks in 2015, have demonstrated how corporations and high-net-worth individuals can effectively organize their wealth and income across borders through the global financial system, utilizing offshore financial centers and various legal business structures. In these instances, corporations engage in what can be described as "tax games" by manipulating profits between different jurisdictions to exploit gaps and discrepancies in tax regulations. They may engage in artificial trading with shell companies within their corporate groups, effectively conducting transactions with themselves, thereby making profits vanish. This can ultimately result in minimal or even zero corporate taxes being paid. Notable individuals, including figures like Lewis Hamilton, the Queen, Bono, and others, have faced criticism for their involvement in such tax avoidance schemes. The level of their culpability varies, whether they were fully aware, willfully blind, or simply ignorant of how these arrangements functioned to their benefit.

However, it is crucial to scrutinize the role played by leading banks, accounting firms, and financial institutions in facilitating these tax arrangements, particularly considering that many of these entities are based in British Overseas Territories, such as Appleby in Bermuda and Estera in the Cayman Islands. Another critical aspect of these schemes involves third-party institutions known as trust and company service providers, including firms like Appleby and Estera, which were the sources of the Paradise Papers leaks. These companies establish and maintain corporate entities to structure artificial or contrived financial arrangements, raising questions about their role in these practices.

How We Envisage Society Functioning

While organizing finances in these ways may be legally permissible, it prompts us to question the ethics of a system that exacerbates wealth inequality globally. This ethical inquiry delves into the fundamental nature of how we envision society functioning. When we focus on the harm tax avoidance inflicts upon society rather than merely adhering to its legal definition, we recognize its contribution to growing inequality and the increased tax burden on ordinary taxpayers. It also erodes the legitimacy of the state. Furthermore, the government's accommodation of structures that facilitate tax avoidance can be exploited by those seeking to conceal illicit funds, as exemplified by significant investments from offshore tax havens into the UK's property market.

Tax avoidance diverts funds away from the public purse, a concern magnified during budgetary austerity and economic uncertainty, and undermines the perception of social fairness. There is an improper transfer of resources away from public goods and services. Despite political rhetoric highlighting the adverse effects of tax avoidance, it must be addressed rigorously. While the UK, with sovereignty over several offshore territories, has made pledges to tackle tax avoidance, punitive enforcement actions have yet to follow suit.

A potential solution could be a unitary tax regime, treating multinational businesses as single entities for tax purposes. However, once there is a legal requirement for all tax avoidance schemes to gain formal state approval before use, rather than being shut down after discovery, room remains for tax entrepreneurs to evade their responsibilities.

Minimizing Tax Liability

Understanding the tax credits and deductions and calculating them correctly can significantly impact your tax liability, potentially leading to a refund instead of owing more money at tax time. Several strategies can help minimize your tax liability:

1. Increase Your Retirement Contributions: One effective way to reduce taxable income is by contributing to an employer-sponsored retirement plan or a traditional individual retirement account (IRA). Employer plans, such as a 401(k) or 403(b), allow you to contribute pre-tax dollars, directly reducing your annual taxable income. Contributions to traditional IRAs also reduce taxable income.
2. Profit From Investment Losses: Selling investments that have decreased value can offset gains or other income up to a specific limit each year, reducing your tax liability. This strategy, known as tax-loss harvesting, allows unused losses to be carried forward to future years.
3. Contribute to Traditional Plans: Consider contributing to traditional 401(k) or 403(b) plans if employer-sponsored plans are unavailable. These contributions are made with pre-tax dollars, directly reducing

taxable income. Traditional IRAs also offer similar benefits.

4. Donate to Charity: Contributions to qualified charitable organizations can reduce your taxes if you itemize deductions on your tax return. Cash or goods donations can qualify, with a receipt required for donations exceeding $250. Deductions for charitable donations can be up to 60% of your adjusted gross income (AGI).

These strategies can help minimize your tax liability, but consulting with a tax professional for personalized guidance and ensuring compliance with tax laws is advisable.

Strategies to Safeguard Your Income from Taxation

Income is subject to taxation at various levels, including federal, state, and local, and additional levies are imposed on earned income to fund Social Security and Medicare. While taxes are inevitable, several strategies are available to mitigate their impact. Here are some key considerations:

Invest in Municipal Bonds: One significant advantage of investing in municipal bonds is that, assuming you hold the bond until maturity, you typically do not have to pay federal, state, or local taxes on the interest income. This tax-free interest makes municipal bonds an appealing option for investors. However, it is essential to note that not all municipal bonds are entirely tax-exempt. If you purchased the bond at a discount exceeding 0.25 percent, a "de minimis" tax may apply, taxing interest and gains from the discounted amount as regular income. Overall, municipal bonds have historically displayed lower default rates than corporate bonds.

Favor Long-Term Capital Gains: Investing in stocks, mutual funds, bonds, and real estate can be instrumental in building wealth. One notable tax advantage of these investments is the preferential treatment of long-term capital gains. If you hold a capital asset for over a year before selling it, you can benefit from a lower tax rate of 0 percent, 15 percent, or 20 percent, depending on your income level. In contrast, short-term capital gains are taxed at ordinary income rates. It is essential to stay updated on the income thresholds determining the applicable capital gains tax rates, as they can change annually. Tax-loss harvesting is also a valuable strategy for offsetting capital gains tax liabilities.

Consider Starting a Business: Running a side business offers additional income and various tax advantages. Many business-related expenses can be deducted from your income, reducing your overall tax liability. This includes home office expenses, which may be eligible for deduction according to IRS guidelines. To claim these deductions, your business activities must demonstrate an intention to generate a profit. Moreover, the Setting Every Community Up for Retirement Enhancement (SECURE) Act of 2019 offers tax incentives to employers participating in multiple-employer retirement plans, benefitting businesses and employees.

Maximize Retirement Contributions and Employee Benefits: Using qualified retirement and employee benefit accounts with pre-tax dollars can significantly lower your taxable income. For instance, in 2024, you can contribute up to $23,000 to a 401(k) or 403(b) plan, with an additional catch-up contribution of $7,500 for those aged 50 and above. Self-employed individuals can also benefit from deductible contributions to traditional IRAs. Also, fringe benefits offered by employers, such as flexible spending accounts and educational assistance programs, can further reduce your taxable income.

Utilize Health Savings Accounts (HSAs): Individuals with high-deductible health insurance plans can leverage HSAs to lower their taxable income. Contributions made through payroll deduction are excluded from taxable income, and direct contributions to an HSA are 100 percent tax-deductible. These contributions can be matched by employers and grow tax-free, with withdrawals for qualified medical expenses also tax-free.

Claim Tax Credits: Tax credits directly reduce the amount of taxes you owe, making them highly valuable. The Child Tax Credit and the Earned Income Tax Credit (EITC) are two commonly claimed credits. The Child Tax Credit can significantly reduce your tax burden, provided you meet income and dependency criteria. The EITC offers substantial benefits for low to lower-middle-income families.

Additional tax credits are available, such as the American Opportunity Tax

Credit and the Saver's Credit, each with specific eligibility requirements. These strategies can help reduce your taxable income and overall tax liability. It is advisable to consult with a tax professional to ensure you maximize available deductions and credits while adhering to tax regulations.

Understanding Business Taxation

Business taxation encompasses the taxes businesses must pay as an integral aspect of their daily operations. Businesses of all types need to adhere to tax regulations, whether you operate as a sole proprietor, a partner in a business partnership, a limited liability company (LLC), or part of a corporation. The tax implications vary depending on your business structure, making it crucial to align your business entity with your financial and operational goals, including succession planning. There are five primary categories of business taxes:

1. Gross-Receipts Tax: This tax is based on a business's total revenue or sales and can vary by locality.
2. Corporate Franchise Tax: Corporations often pay this tax levied on the privilege of doing business in a specific jurisdiction.
3. Employment Withholding Tax: Businesses are responsible for withholding and remitting payroll taxes on behalf of their employees.
4. Excise Tax: Excise taxes are imposed on specific goods, services, or activities, such as alcohol, tobacco, or transportation.
5. Value-Added Tax (VAT): Common in many countries, VAT is a consumption tax applied at each stage of the production and distribution process.

In specific industries like mining and insurance, additional sector-specific taxes may apply. While businesses also contend with income tax, property tax, and sales tax, it is worth noting that these are not exclusive to businesses and impact individuals as well. In essence, all taxes collectively impact individuals at a personal level.

Understanding Tax Liability

As a small business owner, managing various expenses, including taxes, is crucial to your financial responsibilities. Taxation covers various aspects of your business, as mandated by governmental authorities. Your tax liability represents the total amount you owe to federal, state, and local tax agencies. These funds are allocated towards supporting government operations and social programs. It is important to emphasize that tax liability is a legally binding obligation, and failure to fulfill it may lead to government-imposed penalties. This type of liability is categorized as short-term, requiring payment within a year. Your accounting records or balance sheet typically document short-term liabilities, including tax liabilities.

Every transaction with a tax consequence is known as a "taxable event." The government determines which events are subject to taxation. Whenever such an event occurs within your business, you are responsible for paying the corresponding tax to the relevant authority. Taxable events encompass activities like generating income, issuing payroll, and making sales, each of which incurs a specific tax liability calculated as a percentage of the total event. For instance, when you sell a product, the government may impose a sales tax, which you can include in the total price charged to customers. Subsequently, you must report and remit the collected sales tax to the appropriate governmental agencies, typically regularly (e.g., quarterly or monthly). Earning income is another taxable event, with federal and state income tax liability calculated based on a percentage of your earned income.

Calculating Business Taxes

To minimize your tax obligations legally, it is essential to comprehend the intricacies of taxation processes and the precise timing and execution of business and personal transactions. As a business owner and taxpayer, you will often encounter multiple methods to complete a taxable transaction, with one approach resulting in the lowest legal tax liability. It is crucial to differentiate between tax avoidance, a legitimate practice of minimizing tax liability through strategic financial planning, and tax evasion, which is illegal and involves concealing or deceiving authorities to evade taxes. There may be opportunities to deduct business expenses for businesses engaged in a "trade or business" with a profit motive and economic activity. The IRS defines a trade or business as involving profit motives and economic activities.

All taxable income is reported within the context of the tax year; encompassing income received or accrued during that specific year and relevant expenses paid or accrued. Tax-saving strategies should be applied before the end of the tax year to maximize benefits. Furthermore, businesses must disclose their chosen accounting method to the IRS, typically selecting between "cash" and "accrual" methods. In certain situations, hybrid methods combining elements of both may be permitted. Additionally, specific business types may qualify for specialized accounting methods, adding to the complexity of tax considerations.

The Impact of Corporate Taxation on Concentration and Inequality

Corporate concentration has become a prominent issue in the United States, raising debates on its causes, effects, and potential solutions. This article delves into a less-discussed aspect of this debate: corporate taxation. This article unveils a significant tax advantage favoring large domestic and international businesses by conducting the first empirical analysis of effective tax rates (ETRs) for nonfinancial corporations categorized by size and geographical jurisdiction. The analysis also explores how this regressive tax structure intertwines with the growing power of major corporations within the corporate landscape, leading to shifts in firm-level dynamics. As large corporations prioritize shareholder value over investments that might indirectly benefit workers, the corporate tax structure correlates with increasing corporate concentration. It contributes to the widening wealth gap among households.

In recent decades, the largest corporations in the United States have consistently captured larger shares of net income, revenues, assets, and market capitalization. Studies reveal that this concentration has been associated with raising prices, lowering wages, delivering lower-quality products and services, and constraining output. This corporate consolidation has been blamed for sluggish economic growth and declining productivity. Some argue that the United States has lost its competitive edge relative to Europe due to its failure to combat this concentration. Concentration is also linked to rising income inequality and the growing political influence of major corporations. As a result, many people perceive the system as biased towards elites, further fueling populist discontent.

Several factors have driven the dominance of a few "superstar" companies, including globalization and technological changes. Multinationals expand their operations and reduce costs through globalization, while network effects encourage "winner-takes-all" dynamics in technology sectors. Digital platforms, for instance, naturally gravitate towards monopoly as the goal is to connect everyone within a single network. However, concentration is not limited to globalized tech sectors; it has also infiltrated domestically oriented brick-and-mortar industries. This ubiquity of corporate giants suggests that market processes alone cannot explain the phenomenon. Politics and public policy play a substantial role, with regulatory bodies like the Federal Trade Commission and the Department of Justice facing criticism for enabling concentration through lax antitrust policies and merger oversight.

Traditionally, mainstream economists and policymakers downplayed the consequences of corporate concentration, asserting that it reflects the efficiency of large corporations in exploiting economies of scale, ultimately benefiting consumers. However, this view has been increasingly challenged, even within the Chicago School of Economics. Events in recent years, such as conferences addressing antitrust concerns, reflect a shift in perspective. Politicians have also taken note of the political implications of corporate concentration, with both Democrats and Republicans expressing concern. Antitrust policy, dating back to the Sherman Act of 1890 and the Clayton Act of 1914, has historically been the primary tool to combat the power of large corporations. The rollback of robust antitrust measures in recent decades coincided with the rise of concentration, emphasizing the link between the two.

Despite the scrutiny of large corporations' tax practices, there needs to be more examination of the relationship between corporate taxation and concentration. However, research reveals a substantial and persistent tax advantage for big businesses in recent decades. Notably, in the 1970s, the top 10 percent faced consistently higher worldwide ETRs than the bottom 90 percent. However, by the early 1980s, large and small corporations shared a 29 percent ETR. Since the mid-1980s, large corporations have consistently enjoyed lower worldwide ETRs than their smaller counterparts, with the gap widening in recent years (28 percent for the top 10 percent compared to 41 percent for the bottom 90 percent). The study further breaks down these rates into domestic and foreign components, highlighting a significant disparity in domestic ETRs and a shift in foreign ETR progressivity in recent years.

In terms of power dynamics, or using "capital as power," the reduction in the relative tax burden of large corporations since the mid-1980s aligns with an increase in their power, as measured by net profit margins. This reduction also corresponds to transforming power relations within and outside these firms. Income inequality widens as large corporations prioritize shareholder value over investments that might benefit ordinary workers. This underscores the corporate tax structure's interconnectedness with rising corporate concentration and household inequality.

Generally, the decline in corporate tax receipts and the lowering of statutory corporate tax rates have played a significant role in the stagnation of tax revenues over recent decades. This suggests that a substantial portion of the shift from the tax state to the debt state can be attributed to changes in the structure of corporate taxation. Increasing corporate power and decreasing ETRs for large corporations will likely result in reduced relative investments, particularly in areas that drive productivity, innovation, and job creation. This aligns with the "business sabotage" concept, where more giant corporations may prioritize profit maintenance over societal welfare, limiting productivity and innovation. As large corporations gain more power and reduce their ETRs relative to smaller counterparts, they may redirect resources from workers to shareholders and managers. This shift can exacerbate household inequality by increasing shareholder payouts while reducing investments that could lead to job opportunities.

In summary, the persistently regressive worldwide tax structure since the mid-1980s can be attributed to the consistently regressive domestic tax structure and the recent shift towards regressivity in the foreign tax structure. Declining corporate tax progressivity is a defining feature of the evolving debt state over the past few decades.

Taxes, Power, and the Financialization of Corporations

The contemporary rise of shareholder value is a widespread phenomenon in the corporate world. However, it has different effects on power dynamics within large and smaller corporations. The persistent reduction in the relative tax burden of large corporations has not compelled these powerful entities to reinvest their tax savings into productive capacity. On the contrary, empirical evidence suggests that as significant corporations become more oriented toward short-term shareholder value enhancement, which disproportionately benefits the asset-rich, they become less inclined to invest in ways that promote productivity, innovation, and job creation, which would benefit ordinary workers. Consequently, the corporate tax structure is not only linked to corporate concentration but also to the widening inequality within the household sector. While widening income inequality is often attributed to declining progressivity in the individual or personal income tax system, our research highlights the significant role played by corporate taxation as well. Over the past few decades, the persistent regressivity in the worldwide tax structure has provided substantial tax advantages to large corporations, coinciding with an increase in their relative power within the corporate landscape and a shift in power dynamics within and beyond the firm.

The dominant empirical evidence thus underscores the importance of addressing tax-related issues in ongoing discussions about corporate concentration, particularly in the United States. Among other things, a multifaceted approach is essential, encompassing corporate taxation, antitrust measures, and other policies that impact distributive outcomes. Lower corporate taxes may not necessarily benefit the society. Instead, successive corporate tax reforms contribute to a persistently regressive tax structure, and wealth and income continue to concentrate at the top. Progressive corporate tax may help rectify some of the significant power imbalances that have emerged under the debt state paradigm.

Review Questions

1. What is the critical advantage of tax-free income, and what are some sources of tax-free earnings?
2. Explain the concept of tax deferral and its benefits for individuals.
3. What are the essential elements of legal compliance in tax planning, and why is staying informed crucial?
4. Distinguish between tax avoidance and tax evasion, and discuss the ethical considerations surrounding tax avoidance.
5. What strategies can individuals use to minimize tax liability, and why is consulting with a tax professional recommended?
6. How does the corporate tax structure affect income inequality, and what role does taxation play in the concentration of corporate power?

Discussion Points

1. The Balance Between Legal Compliance and Ethical Responsibility: Discuss the delicate balance between legal tax avoidance and ethical considerations. When does tax avoidance become unethical?
2. Corporate Taxation and Concentration: Explore the connection between corporate taxation policies and large corporations' concentration of power and wealth.
3. The Impact of Tax Structure on Income Inequality: Discuss how the evolving tax structure, especially for large corporations, can contribute to income inequality and its societal implications.

CHAPTER FOUR: STRATEGIES AND IMPLICATIONS OF CORPORATE TAX MANAGEMENT

Summary of Key Points

1. Definition and Functioning of Corporate Tax: Corporate tax is a levy on a corporation's profit, calculated after subtracting allowable expenses from revenue. This tax is a significant source of government revenue and varies by country, with special considerations for deductions and effective rates.

2. Corporate Tax Deductions: Corporations can reduce taxable income through necessary and ordinary business expenses, including operational costs, employee benefits, and investments, which are critical for tax planning and financial decision-making.

3. Special Considerations in Corporate Taxation: Issues like double taxation and the option for businesses to elect S corporation status illustrate the complexity of corporate tax laws and their implications for business structure and shareholder taxation.

4. Benefits and Strategic Tax Planning: Paying corporate taxes offers benefits like deductible expenses and loss deductions, influencing corporate financial strategies, including investment and operational decisions.

5. Impact of Global Tax Systems: Differences in national tax systems add complexity to multinational enterprises' financial management, requiring strategic planning to navigate compliance costs and double

taxation risks.

6. Future Trends and Case Studies in Tax Management: The evolving global tax landscape, with initiatives like the CCCTB and digital services taxes, underscores the importance of strategic tax management and adaptation to regulatory changes.

Corporate Tax: Definition, Deductions, and Functioning

Corporate tax is a levy placed on the profit of a corporation. The taxable income for a corporation is calculated by subtracting various expenses from its revenue. These expenses include the cost of goods sold (COGS), general and administrative (G&A) expenses, selling and marketing costs, research and development expenditures, depreciation, and other operating costs. The corporate tax rate varies across countries, and some nations are known as tax havens due to their meager tax rates. The actual tax rate paid by a corporation, known as the effective corporate tax rate, often differs from the statutory rate (the official rate before deductions) due to various deductions, government subsidies, and tax loopholes. Key points to note about corporate taxes are the following:

1. Corporate taxes are a significant source of government revenue.
2. The tax base for corporations is determined after deducting eligible expenses.
3. In the United States, the corporate tax rate is a flat 21 percent since the Tax Cuts and Jobs Act (TCJA) of 2017, a reduction from the previous 35 percent.

Corporations can avoid double taxation as their income passes directly to business owners, who report it on their tax returns. Under the Corporate Tax Since the TCJA passed in 2017 under President Donald Trump, the federal corporate tax rate in the U.S. has been flat at 21 percent. Corporate tax returns in the U.S. are generally due by the 15th day of the fourth month following the end of the corporation's fiscal year. Corporations can request a six-month extension and have installment payment due dates for estimated taxes in April, June, September, and December. The IRS requires corporations to report taxes on Form 1120; those with assets over $10 million must file electronically. Additionally, several states in the U.S. impose their corporate income taxes, with rates varying significantly.

Corporate Tax Deductions: Corporations can lower their taxable income through necessary and ordinary business expenditures. These include operational expenses, investments, and income-generating real estate purchases. Deductible expenses include employee salaries, health benefits, tuition reimbursements, bonuses, insurance premiums, travel expenses, bad debts, interest payments, and various taxes like sales, fuel, and excise taxes. Furthermore, tax preparation, legal services, bookkeeping, and advertising costs can also reduce taxable income.

Special Considerations - Double Taxation and S Corporations: A notable issue in corporate taxation is double taxation, where the company's profits are taxed, and then dividends distributed to shareholders are also taxed individually. To avoid this, some businesses register as S corporations, where income is passed directly to owners and taxed on their returns, bypassing corporate taxation.

Benefits of Paying Corporate Tax: Corporate taxes can offer advantages over additional individual income tax. These include deductions for medical insurance and fringe benefits like retirement plans. Corporations can also fully deduct losses, whereas sole proprietors face more stringent requirements. Profits retained within the corporation can be used for tax planning, potentially leading to future tax benefits.

Corporate Tax and Financial Decision-Making: Financial managers of all sizes aim to optimize tax liabilities, considering location, organizational form, and transaction types. However, tax planning strategies can sometimes distort financial decisions, especially in multinational companies, where the heterogeneity of national tax systems and unequal treatment of debt and equity can lead to various distortions.

Impact of Diverse National Tax Systems: The differences in national tax codes add complexity to the financial management of international groups, leading to high compliance costs and double taxation risks, particularly in transfer pricing and international group restructuring. In response, some governments and organizations propose systems like international tax consolidation or consolidation and formulary appropriation to tax the economic reality of multinational enterprises rather than just their legal entities.

Future Trends in Corporate Tax Planning: The shift to systems like the Common Consolidated Corporate Tax Base (CCCTB) in the EU could significantly impact corporate tax planning strategies. Recent research explores the behavior of multinational enterprises under various tax environments, focusing on investment distribution and internal debt use. Interestingly, specific international tax consolidation systems, like those in Denmark, France, Italy, and Austria, give taxing rights to the parent company's country, offering alternative approaches to taxing international consolidated income.

In summary, corporate tax is a complex but crucial aspect of a corporation's financial planning and legal compliance. Businesses need to understand its workings, including deductions, rates, and special considerations like S corporations and double taxation. The evolving landscape of international tax laws and consolidation systems also poses challenges and opportunities for multinational enterprises in their tax planning strategies.

Industry-Specific Examples of Effective Tax Management

Technology Sector – Apple Inc.: Apple is a prime example of effective international tax planning. The company skillfully structures its operations to take advantage of favorable tax jurisdictions and employs legal strategies to optimize its global tax position. This case underscores the importance of strategic tax planning for multinational corporations.

Consumer Goods – Procter & Gamble (P&G): P&G integrates its tax management strategy with its business focus on innovation. The company leverages tax incentives for research and development, benefiting from tax credits and deductions that align with its innovative product development goals.

Financial Services - JPMorgan Chase: JPMorgan Chase demonstrates expertise in managing tax liabilities by optimizing its corporate structure. This approach showcases how financial institutions can navigate complex tax regulations to effectively utilize available deductions and credits.

Lessons and Strategies for Success

Strategic Alignment: Effective tax management should harmonize with a company's overall business strategy, supporting goals like global expansion, innovation, or enhancing operational efficiency.

Regulatory Adaptability: As tax laws and regulations evolve, successful companies proactively adapt their tax strategies to stay compliant and seize new opportunities.

Proactive Risk Management: Performing comprehensive risk assessments is a critical practice in tax management, enabling businesses to proactively anticipate and address potential challenges.

Commitment to Transparency: A transparent approach in reporting tax strategies and compliance efforts builds trust among stakeholders and enhances the company's reputation.

Embracing Technological Advancements: Implementing technology in tax management through automation and data analytics is crucial for process efficiency and informed decision-making.

Illustrative Case Study

ABC Pharma, a multinational pharmaceutical company, showcases successful tax management through strategic planning. The company aligns its tax approach with its emphasis on research and development, making it eligible for tax credits. By structuring its international operations strategically, ABC Pharma effectively utilizes tax treaties and optimizes transfer pricing, thus minimizing double taxation risks. The company's transparent reporting on its tax strategies in its annual reports and CSR disclosures solidifies stakeholder trust.

These case studies highlight the significance of strategic alignment, adaptability to regulatory changes, risk management, transparency, and technological integration in effective tax management, contributing to long-term financial health.

Future Trends in Tax Management

Changing Tax Regulatory Environment

1. Taxation of Digital Transactions: There is a growing global focus on taxing digital transactions and services, with initiatives like the European Union's Digital Services Tax targeting major tech companies to ensure fair tax distribution in the digital economy.
2. Environmental Tax Initiatives: Governments increasingly incorporate environmental factors into their tax policies. Taxes like carbon taxes encourage eco-friendly business practices and support global climate change efforts.
3. Unified Global Tax Framework: Organizations like the OECD spearhead the movement towards a more cohesive global taxation system. This includes efforts to combat profit shifting and establish a global minimum corporate tax rate.
4. Advancements in Digital Tax Administration: Tax authorities are integrating technologies such as AI and blockchain to enhance tax processes' efficiency, transparency, and compliance.

Implications and Approaches for Businesses

1. Navigating Compliance Challenges: Companies operating in multiple countries must be prepared to adapt to legislative changes and engage with tax authorities proactively.
2. Investing in Digital Capabilities: In an era of digital transformation, businesses need to invest in technology to manage tax processes effectively

and comply with evolving regulations.

Future Outlook

As the focus on digital taxation and environmental policies intensifies, multinational corporations must recalibrate their tax strategies accordingly. A proactive approach towards adopting green policies and investing in technological advancements will be critical to effectively managing future tax challenges.

In summary, digitalization, environmental policies, and global tax cooperation will influence the evolving landscape of tax management. Businesses must stay agile, embrace technological advancements, and actively participate in global tax discussions to navigate these changes successfully.

Impact of Tax Discrimination between Debt and Equity on Corporate Capital Structure

The varied tax treatment of debt and equity creates a significant distortion in the capital structure of companies. Most tax systems favor debt over equity by allowing tax deductions for interest payments, whereas returns to shareholders like retained earnings or dividends are not tax-deductible. This leads companies to weigh financing options based on their tax implications, often resulting in a preference for debt. The 2008 financial crisis highlighted the risks of excessive reliance on debt, particularly in the banking sector, where over-leverage led to instability and defaults. This issue was not limited to banks; many firms faced financial distress due to a tax system that incentivized debt financing over equity. Post-crisis, policymakers began exploring reforms to mitigate such vulnerabilities, including adopting an Allowance for Corporate Equity and a Comprehensive Business Income Tax. These reforms aim to equalize the tax treatment of debt and equity financing. While some countries like Italy, Brazil, Austria, and Croatia have implemented versions of the Allowance for Corporate Equity, the effectiveness of these measures remains a topic of debate.

The Belgian Experience - Risk Capital Deduction: Since January 1, 2006, Belgian companies have been able to deduct a "Risk Capital Deduction" from their taxable income, equalizing the tax treatment of debt and equity. This measure, intended to promote equity-funded activities and strengthen capital structures, allows companies to deduct a fictitious interest cost of their adjusted equity. The deduction includes new and existing equity, calculated annually based on the average return of 10-year state bonds two years prior. The introduction of the Allowance for Corporate Equity in Belgium had dual objectives: to make capital structure decisions more tax-neutral and to retain multinational companies by offering a tax advantage equivalent to the abolished special regime for coordination centers. The reform decreased debt ratios by 2 to 7 percent among companies, indicating its effectiveness. However, the reform benefited large corporations more than small and medium enterprises, suggesting continued favoritism towards multinational firms.

While aiming for tax neutrality, the Belgian model has faced criticism for favoring multinational enterprises and being costly for public finances without clear evidence of boosting the economy or employment. A possible solution could be combining the Allowance for Corporate Equity with a Comprehensive Business Income Tax, providing equal but limited tax deductibility for debt and equity costs. Another challenge is the measure's cost-effectiveness. The tax advantage can be availed without generating new investments since it considers both new and existing equity. This aspect might be seen as a policy shortcoming, particularly in times of fiscal consolidation.

Generally, varying tax environments offer multinational enterprises numerous profit-shifting opportunities. Additionally, tax relief methods like the credit method for cross-border dividends could lead to more efficient financial solutions and eliminate profit-shifting incentives. Also, experience from Belgium's 2006 tax reform shows that traditional tax systems encourage higher debt usage than systems with equal tax treatment for debt and equity. The results also suggest that larger companies are more influenced by the equity tax shield than smaller firms. While the Allowance for Corporate Equity in Belgium made capital structure decisions more tax-neutral, a

Comprehensive Business Income Tax that disallows debt interest deductions could achieve similar results at a lower cost. However, the study found no definitive impact of this reform on investment decisions, indicating that further analysis and policy adjustments might be necessary.

The Principles of Proactive Tax Planning: Essential Considerations for Business Owners

In the bustling world of business management, tax planning often needs to be more balanced. However, proactive tax planning is a crucial element of strategic business operations. Neglecting this aspect can put your business at a disadvantage compared to competitors. If you still need to focus on proactive tax planning, now is the time to start. Here are five key areas to consider for impactful business tax planning:

Review Your Accounting Methods: Evaluate whether you are paying taxes on earnings you have yet to receive. Suppose your business has less than $25 million in average gross receipts over three years. In that case, you might be eligible to switch from accrual to cash-basis accounting, potentially offering significant tax savings.

Strategic Planning for Capital Purchases: Consider the timing of major purchases like equipment or vehicles. Utilize accelerated depreciation options available through Section 179 or bonus depreciation to lower your tax bill. Smaller purchases under $2,500 (or up to $5,000 in certain circumstances) can be expensed immediately. If you are not planning new purchases, consider a cost segregation study on existing property to maximize depreciation benefits.

Interim Planning and Quarterly Estimates: Regular income review can help you manage tax positions effectively. Adjusting quarterly tax payments based on income projections helps avoid penalties and manage cash flow. New state-level opportunities also exist to pay taxes as an entity, allowing full deduction of state taxes.

Leveraging Tax Credits: Often overlooked, tax credits can significantly reduce tax liabilities. Look into credits related to hiring practices, research and development, eco-friendly initiatives, and more. The Employee Retention

Tax Credit, for instance, offers substantial benefits.

Succession Planning: Though often a challenging topic, succession planning is vital. It involves more than preparing for unexpected transitions; it encompasses retirement contributions, exit strategies, and estate planning. Proper planning can save on unnecessary taxes in the future.

The above five areas are just the beginning. Tax laws are complex and constantly evolving, so working with a knowledgeable team of advisors is crucial. They can help navigate the tax landscape, ensuring your business remains in the most advantageous position.

Aligning Supply Chain and Tax Strategies

Despite 45 percent of tax executives not being involved in supply chain planning, aligning these strategies is essential for the following reasons:

1. Balancing Operational and Tax Efficiency: Collaboration between tax and operational leaders ensures tax-efficient supply chain decisions. Investing in tax technology and training enables tax departments to provide strategic insights, enhancing overall business efficiency.

2. Optimizing Total Tax Liability: Strategic planning can help achieve tax savings and avoid unexpected tax liabilities, especially during operational changes like onshoring or relocating assets.

3. Managing Tax Compliance Risks: With increased scrutiny from tax authorities, aligning transfer pricing policies with business practices is crucial to avoid disputes and double taxation. Anticipating changes in global tax rules can help avert disadvantageous supply chain strategies.

4. Future-Proofing Tax Structure: A proactive approach in adjusting your tax structure in line with significant business decisions can save time and resources in the long run. Creating a playbook for tax adjustments during significant operational changes is recommended.

In times of economic uncertainty and potential recessions, businesses considering changes in their supply chain will benefit from integrated tax and supply chain strategies. This alignment ensures increased efficiency and competitive advantages, setting them up for long-term success.

Balancing Risk and Reward in Decision-Making

Understanding risk management is crucial for making informed decisions in business. Risk management involves identifying, assessing, and responding to potential threats and opportunities affecting your goals. It includes planning and controlling risk sources and impacts and learning from outcomes. Effective risk management reduces uncertainty, prevents losses, and capitalizes on opportunities.

Risk management is vital for evidence-based, logical decision-making. It aligns actions with values, vision, and mission, improving performance, efficiency, and credibility. It also helps businesses navigate change, complexity, and volatility.

1. Identifying and Assessing Risks: The first step is pinpointing potential risks to your project or business. Tools like SWOT, PESTLE analysis, and risk matrices help evaluate the likelihood and impact of risks, considering their sources, causes, consequences, stakeholders, resources, and constraints.

2. Responding to Risks: After identifying risks, decide how to respond. Options include avoiding, reducing, transferring, or accepting risks. Avoiding eliminates the risk source, reducing and minimizes its likelihood or impact, transferring shifts the risk to another party, and accepting acknowledges the risk and its potential consequences.

3. Monitoring and Controlling Risks: Once you have responded to risks, continuously monitor and control them. Track the effectiveness of your responses, adapt to changes in the risk environment, and regularly update your risk register and plans. Implement corrective actions and contingency plans as needed.

4. Learning from Risks: Finally, learn from managed risks through reviews or lessons learned sessions. Document findings and best practices, applying them to future endeavors.

The Current Climate of Risk for Businesses

Today's business landscape presents unprecedented challenges, including inflation, regional conflicts, public scrutiny, regulatory complexity, supply chain issues, and financial market instability. Such risks demand corporate leaders to invest in innovation for competitiveness and resilience.

Innovation as a Mitigation Tool: Innovative solutions help address these risks. Leaders invest in staff training and new technologies to streamline processes and enhance competitiveness. Embracing innovation, especially in technology, is crucial for long-term success.

Overcoming Innovation Barriers: Budget constraints, lack of expertise, and internal resistance are common barriers to innovation. To overcome these, businesses should:

1. Evaluate the impact of risks on short- and long-term goals.
2. Understand motivations for innovation.
3. Utilize modern technologies and partner effectively.
4. Research new technologies thoroughly.
5. Identify and address internal and external innovation barriers.
6. Keep customer-centric strategies at the forefront.

The Path to Innovation

The journey towards innovation, while challenging, offers more significant potential than maintaining the status quo. In a world of constant change, proactive investment in innovation and risk management is critical to shaping a successful future.

Review Questions

1. How does the corporate tax rate in the United States compare to other countries, and what was its significant change after the Tax Cuts and Jobs Act of 2017?

2. What types of expenses can be deducted from a corporation's taxable income?
3. How does double taxation affect corporations and shareholders, and what are S corporations?
4. What are the benefits of corporate tax payment for businesses in terms of deductions and tax planning?
5. How do differences in national tax systems affect multinational corporations' financial management and tax planning strategies?
6. Discuss the role of strategic tax planning in navigating the future trends of the global tax regulatory environment.

Discussion Points

1. The Role of Tax Havens: Explore the ethical and economic implications of corporations using tax havens for tax planning and the impact on global tax equity.
2. Digital Transactions and Environmental Taxes: Discuss how the taxation of digital transactions and the introduction of environmental taxes reflect changes in global economic activities and priorities.
3. Balancing Tax Efficiency and Compliance: Consider corporations' challenges in optimizing tax liabilities while ensuring compliance with increasingly complex and diverse global tax regulations.

CHAPTER FIVE: MASTERING TAX PLANNING: STRATEGIES FOR MAXIMIZING SAVINGS

Summary of Key Points

1. Understanding Tax Planning: Tax planning is a strategic approach to reducing tax liabilities and optimizing financial outcomes by utilizing legal deductions, credits, and exemptions. It involves comprehensive planning and understanding tax laws to make informed decisions aligning with financial goals.

2. The Tax Planning Process: The process includes collecting financial data, selecting optimal tax strategies from a broad database, generating tax savings reports, and implementing chosen strategies with the guidance of tax professionals.

3. Principles of Effective Tax Planning: Core principles include compliance with tax laws, maximizing tax benefits through lawful deductions, minimizing tax burdens, maintaining accurate records, and actively seeking tax-saving opportunities.

4. Key Taxes and Their Impact: Understanding different types of taxes—such as income, property, capital gains, inheritance, corporation, VAT, and national insurance—is crucial for effective tax planning.

5. Optimal Timing for Tax Planning: Strategic tax planning involves timing financial decisions and actions at the start of the financial year, mid-year review, year-end, and during significant life events to maximize

tax benefits.

6. Tax Planning for Individuals and Businesses: Strategies include maximizing deductible expenses, making pension contributions, utilizing tax reliefs and allowances, and investing in tax-efficient vehicles tailored to individual or business financial situations.

Tax Planning Process

Tax planning differs from tax compliance. It involves strategic actions to save taxes, like changing business structures, investing in rental properties, or contributing to superannuation. Steps in the tax planning process:

1. Information Gathering: Collect data on group members, income, expenses, assets, and liabilities.
2. Selecting Tax Strategies: Using a database of over 250 strategies, select up to 10 optimal strategies based on unique circumstances.
3. Tax Savings Report: Detail tax savings from selected strategies and provide an implementation plan.
4. Discussion and Implementation: Discuss the report with clients and assist with strategy implementation.

Tax planning is a proactive approach to managing taxes and making intelligent financial decisions. It considers various factors like income sources, investments, and potential deductions to optimize tax positions and align with long-term goals. Effective tax planning is essential for achieving financial stability and success, and it requires understanding basic principles, benefits, strategies, and the value of partnering with a tax professional.

Tax Planning for Individuals and Business Owners

Understanding tax planning is crucial for efficiently managing your finances, whether you are an individual or a business owner. The UK tax system, with its complex laws, rules, and processes, necessitates a focus on three key areas:

basic principles of tax planning, types of taxes, and the optimal timing for tax planning. Tax planning rests on several core principles:

1. Tax Compliance: Adhering to HMRC rules ensures accurate tax payment and avoidance of penalties.
2. Maximizing Tax Benefits: Utilize allowances, deductions, exemptions, and reliefs to optimize your tax position.
3. Minimizing Tax Burdens: Employ lawful methods to reduce the amount of tax owed.
4. Record-Keeping: Keep accurate and comprehensive records for compliance and supporting claims.
5. Active Planning: Regularly review finances and plan strategically to identify tax-saving opportunities.

Knowing the various taxes and their impact on your finances is essential. Key tax types include:

1. Income Tax: Applied to salaries, self-employment earnings, dividends, rental income, and investment gains, with rates based on different tax brackets.
2. Property Tax: Stamp Duty Land Tax (SDLT) levied on property acquisitions.
3. Capital Gains Tax (CGT): Taxed on profits from asset sales.
4. Inheritance Tax: Imposed on asset transfers after death.
5. Corporation Tax: Paid on company profits, with rates varying by business size.
6. Value Added Tax (VAT): A consumption tax on goods and services.
7. National Insurance: Paid on income and profits by employees, employers, and self-employed individuals.

Effective tax management requires considering the timing of financial decisions. Critical times for tax planning decisions include:

1. Start of Financial Year: Begin planning to align financial and tax-saving goals in April.
2. Mid-Year Tax Review: Assess finances to maximize tax benefits and address any issues.
3. Year-End Planning: Utilize last-minute strategies to reduce the current year's tax burden.
4. Life Events: Consider tax implications of marriage, childbirth, home purchases, or starting a business.

Tax planning can significantly enhance your financial flexibility, allowing for savings towards significant purchases, retirement, or business expansion. Key benefits include increased savings, reduced tax obligations, business advantages, asset protection, and decreased risk of penalties and audits. Effective tax planning strategies include claiming legitimate expenses, making pension contributions, utilizing tax reliefs, capitalizing on allowances, and investing in tax-efficient vehicles. Starting your tax planning journey involves:

1. Evaluating Financial Position: Understand your current financial status.
2. Gaining Knowledge: Familiarize yourself with applicable tax laws and updates.
3. Setting Clear Goals: Define your tax planning objectives.
4. Seeking Expert Guidance: Consult with tax professionals for personalized advice.
5. Streamlining Paperwork: Organize all relevant financial documents.
6. Examining Spending: Identify deductible expenses.
7. Reviewing and Adjusting: Regularly update your tax strategies in response to law changes or personal circumstances.

Moreover, collaborating with a tax advisor or accountant ensures expert guidance tailored to your unique financial situation. This partnership helps navigate tax laws, uncover saving opportunities, and ensure ongoing compliance and optimization of your tax position. When planning for taxes, it's essential to consider several critical factors. Firstly, stay informed about current tax laws and regulations. Identifying potential deductions and credits is crucial.

Additionally, evaluate various investment strategies to maximize tax efficiency. Secondly, common mistakes in tax planning can significantly impact your financial situation. These include not planning, failing to keep up with tax law changes, overlooking potential deductions and credits, ignoring long-term financial objectives, and not seeking expert advice. Avoiding these pitfalls can lower your tax liability and improve your financial health.

Available Tax Allowances and Reliefs

Tax allowances and reliefs depend on individual circumstances. They can include personal allowances, specific expense deductions, tax credits for certain activities, and capital gains exemptions. Consulting with an accountant is advisable to determine which allowances and reliefs apply to you. Critical documents for effective tax planning include personal information, income documentation, expense records, investment statements, pension and retirement account details, and tax correspondences.

Tax Planning Strategies for Small Business Owners

Several strategies can aid tax planning for UK-based small business owners or self-employed individuals. These include maximizing tax-deductible business expenses, contributing to pension schemes, and utilizing available tax reliefs and allowances. Consulting a tax advisor or accountant can provide personalized advice based on your situation and goals.

Tax Planning vs Tax Compliance: Tax compliance involves meeting legal obligations and reporting. Tax planning assesses individual circumstances against various strategies to achieve maximum savings. It involves legal deductions, exemptions, structured finances, and tax-effective investing, each with a specific implementation process.

Effective Tax Planning for Dairy Producers: Given the fluctuating prices for inputs like feed, fertilizer, and fuel, dairy producers facing higher taxable income due to solid milk prices must prioritize tax planning. Good record-keeping and timely planning are vital for optimizing tax liabilities. Utilize cash-based reporting to manage income and expenses effectively. Early tax planning, typically around November, allows for accurate income and expense projections, facilitating strategic tax liability adjustments.

Tax Credits vs. Deductions

Tax deductions reduce taxable income, whereas tax credits directly lower tax liability. Both have unique eligibility requirements, including income thresholds. Knowing about life changes that could affect eligibility for these tax breaks is essential.

1. Tax Deduction Types - There are above-the-line deductions (like student loan interest and retirement account contributions) and below-the-line deductions (mortgage interest and medical expenses). The choice between taking the standard deduction or itemizing depends on which offers more significant savings.
2. Types of Tax Credits - Tax credits come in three forms: refundable, partially refundable, and nonrefundable. Refundable credits can result in a tax refund exceeding the amount paid, while nonrefundable credits only reduce the tax bill to zero.

Maximizing the benefits of tax credits and deductions requires understanding their relevance to your personal or business circumstances. Tax preparation software or professional tax advisors can assist in determining eligibility and calculating their impact on your tax bill.

Tax Avoidance vs Tax Evasion

Tax avoidance legally minimizes income tax owed, typically achieved by claiming allowable deductions and credits. This can also include investing in tax-advantaged vehicles like tax-free municipal bonds. Unlike tax evasion, which involves illegal practices such as underreporting income, tax avoidance utilizes lawful methods. Unlike tax evasion, tax avoidance does not involve illegal practices. Tax avoidance is a lawful strategy many taxpayers use to legally reduce their tax bills to the IRS. It includes various credits, deductions, exclusions, and loopholes. For example, claiming the child tax credit, contributing to retirement accounts, or utilizing mortgage tax deductions are forms of tax avoidance. These measures must be legislated into the U.S. Tax Code to influence behavior or support national goals like healthcare or energy efficiency. The complexity of the U.S. Tax Code, partly due to its many tax avoidance provisions, makes it difficult for taxpayers to utilize all available tax breaks. This complexity impacts families and businesses' retirement, savings, and education decision-making. Proposals for Tax Code reform often focus on reducing tax avoidance provisions and simplifying the process.

Types of Tax Avoidance

There are various legal methods of tax avoidance, including:

1. Standard Deduction: Many taxpayers opt for the standard deduction over itemizing.
2. Retirement Savings: Contributing to traditional or Roth retirement plans is a form of tax avoidance.
3. Workplace Expenses: Claiming unreimbursed work-related expenses can be a form of tax avoidance in some states.
4. Offshoring: Corporations and high-net-worth individuals often use offshore tax havens to reduce tax liabilities legally.

Tax evasion involves the deliberate failure to comply with tax laws, such as hiding income or falsifying records, and can result in severe penalties. Tax avoidance is legal when using the tax system's provisions like credits, deductions, and exclusions. However, deliberate disregard for tax laws in avoidance strategies can lead to illegal practices.

Why Tax-Efficient Investing Is Crucial

Investments inherently come with various costs, including commissions, administrative fees, and, notably, taxes, which often significantly reduce returns. However, tax-efficient investing can substantially lessen your tax burden and enhance your overall financial gains, which benefits retirement savings and income generation. The key points to note about tax-efficient investing are:

1. Taxes can substantially reduce the returns on investments.
2. The importance of tax-efficient investing escalates with higher tax brackets.
3. Tax-efficient investments are suitable for taxable accounts.
4. Less tax-efficient investments are preferable for tax-deferred or tax-exempt accounts.
5. Tax-advantaged accounts like IRAs and 401(k)s are subject to annual contribution limits.

Investment types vary in their tax efficiency. For instance, tax-managed funds and ETFs are generally more tax-efficient, while actively managed funds may generate more taxable capital gains. Bonds differ in tax efficiency; municipal bonds offer significant tax advantages, making them suitable for taxable accounts, while corporate bonds are better suited for tax-advantaged accounts. A balanced approach involves holding taxable and tax-advantaged accounts to enjoy the benefits of each. However, the focus should always be on investment selection and asset allocation, tailored to individual circumstances and goals. This strategy aims to maximize returns by reducing tax losses, which is suitable for different accounts. Understanding the tax implications of each investment and account type is crucial. Consultation with financial or investment professionals is advised for personalized guidance.

1. 401(k) Tax Benefits: The key tax advantage of a 401(k) plan is that contributions are pretax, reducing taxable income for the year and

potentially leading to a lower tax bill. However, contributions must stay within annual limits to avoid extra fees and taxes.

2. 401(k) Contribution Limits for 2023: In 2023, the maximum contribution to a 401(k) is $22,500, with an additional $7,500 allowed for those aged 50 or over. In 2024, these limits increase to $23,000 and $7,500, respectively.

Investment choices and asset allocation are vital in influencing returns, but minimizing taxes also plays a crucial role. Tax-efficient investing is essential because:

1. Taxes paid are immediate financial losses.
2. The potential growth of taxed money, if invested, is lost.

Considering after-tax returns is essential since these funds are available for spending now and in retirement. To optimize returns and retain more earnings, embracing tax-efficient investing is critical.

Tax-efficient investing involves selecting appropriate investments and accounts for holding them. The primary account types include taxable and tax-advantaged accounts, each with benefits and limitations.

Taxable Accounts and Tax-Advantaged Accounts

Taxable accounts offer no specific tax benefits, like brokerage accounts, but provide more flexibility than tax-advantaged accounts. For instance, funds in a brokerage account can be withdrawn anytime without tax penalties. Taxation on returns depends on the holding period of the investment. Tax-advantaged accounts include tax-deferred accounts like traditional IRAs and 401(k)s, offering upfront tax breaks, and tax-exempt accounts like Roth IRAs and Roth 401(k)s, where investments grow tax-free, and qualified retirement withdrawals are tax-free. However, these accounts come with restrictions on withdrawals.

Strategies for Tax-Efficient Investing: Given annual contribution limits to

IRAs and 401(k)s and their withdrawal restrictions, not all investments can be ideally placed in tax-advantaged accounts. A strategic approach is placing tax-efficient investments in taxable and less tax-efficient investments in tax-advantaged accounts.

In summary, minimizing taxes is a fundamental principle of investing, whether for retirement savings or cash generation. Tax-efficient investments in appropriate accounts can optimize growth over time. However, investors may sometimes need to prioritize factors other than taxes. Consulting a qualified investment planner or tax specialist is crucial for tailored tax strategy advice.

Understanding Tax-Exempt Interest

Tax-exempt interest is interest income exempt from federal income tax. Sometimes, the amount of tax-exempt interest can affect eligibility for other tax benefits. Familiar sources include municipal bonds and assets in Roth retirement accounts. Critical points on tax-exempt interest include:

1. Tax-exempt interest is not subject to federal income tax.
2. Some municipal bonds offer triple tax exemption (federal, state, local).
3. Tax-exempt interest is also earned in Roth retirement accounts and certain tax-advantaged products.

Tax-exempt interest is often misunderstood as it might still be subjected to state or local taxation and possibly the alternative minimum tax (AMT). Only the interest from certain investments, like municipal bonds, is tax-exempt, not the capital gains from these investments. A common way to earn federally tax-exempt interest is through municipal bonds, primarily if the bonds are issued in the investor's state or locality of residence.

Municipal Bonds and Tax Implications: Municipal bonds are a typical source of tax-exempt interest. However, the tax-exempt status at the federal level does not necessarily apply to state taxes. For example, a California resident owning a New York municipal bond would owe California state tax on the interest. Tax laws differ across states, with some taxing interest on all municipal bonds and others exempting in-state bonds.

Triple-Tax-Exempt Investments

An investment described as triple-tax-exempt is usually a municipal bond exempt from municipal, state, and federal taxes.

State and Local Taxation on Interest: The IRS notes that interest on state or local government obligations can be tax-exempt, even if the obligation is not in the form of a bond. This includes interest on ordinary written agreements or default interest paid by an insurer on behalf of the state or local government.

Mutual Funds with Tax-Exempt Interest: Mutual funds holding a mix of stocks and municipal bonds may earn a portion of tax-exempt interest. The federal tax exemption applies to earnings from bonds and may also extend to state taxes, depending on the origin of the bonds and the investor's residency.

Impact on Adjusted Gross Income (AGI): Tax-exempt interest is not factored into AGI calculations for tax purposes. Payers of over $10 in tax-exempt interest must report it to taxpayers and the IRS on Form 1099-INT, and taxpayers must report this interest on Form 1040. This reported that the IRS uses interest to determine the taxable portion of Social Security benefits.

Understanding Retirement Contributions

A retirement contribution is a monetary deposit into a retirement plan. Depending on the retirement plan's qualification status, these contributions can be either pretax or after-tax. Annual limits are set on how much can be contributed to these accounts, and qualified contributions offer tax benefits under certain conditions. The critical points on retirement contributions include:

1. Retirement contributions are funds designated for qualified retirement accounts like IRAs and 401(k)s.
2. Contributions can be pretax (for traditional IRAs and 401(k)s) or after-

tax (for Roth accounts).

3. The IRS sets annual limits for contributions to retirement accounts.

Contributions can be made into various retirement accounts, including traditional and Roth IRAs, 401(k)s, 403(b)s, and 457 plans. The choice of account type depends on the individual's circumstances, and some may have multiple accounts, like a 401(k) and an IRA. The IRS sets annual limits on retirement contributions. For 2023, the limit for 401(k) plans is $22,500, increasing to $23,000 in 2024, with an additional catch-up contribution for those aged 50 or over. SIMPLE plan limits are $15,500 for 2023, rising to $16,000 in 2024, with a catch-up contribution available. IRA contribution limits are $6,500 for 2023 and $7,000 for 2024, with a $1,000 catch-up contribution for those 50 or older.

Contributing at least 10 percent of income and diversifying investments increases the likelihood of a substantial retirement fund. Conversely, inadequate contributions or overly conservative investments can lead to insufficient funds in retirement. Employer contributions, often in the form of matching funds, are essential to many retirement plans, supplementing individual contributions.

Tax Status of Retirement Contributions: Retirement contributions to plans like 401(k)s might be tax-deferred, meaning taxes are not paid on the contributed amounts until withdrawal. Contributions can also be made with either pretax or after-tax funds, affecting when taxes are paid on retirement earnings.

Pretax Contributions: Pretax contributions, typical in 401(k) plans, offer immediate tax benefits by reducing taxable income in the contribution year. This can incentivize employees to save for retirement. Ideally, the income tax rate during retirement will be lower than during working years, making pretax contributions advantageous despite future taxes on earnings.

After-Tax Contributions: After-tax contributions, where taxes are paid on the money before it is contributed, appeal to those expecting higher tax rates in retirement. Roth IRAs and 401(k)s exemplify after-tax retirement products, offering tax-free growth of investment earnings and tax-free withdrawals in retirement.

Pretax vs. After-Tax Contributions: Choosing between pretax and Roth contributions depends on comparing current and expected retirement tax brackets. For example, pretax contributions might be more beneficial if expecting a lower tax rate in retirement. Conversely, if expecting a higher rate, Roth contributions could be advantageous. Diversifying retirement savings across both Roth and pretax accounts can offer flexibility in managing taxable income during retirement.

History of Retirement Contributions

Historically, pensions were the mainstay of America's retirement system, with a significant shift occurring in the 1980s towards 401(k) plans. Unlike pensions guaranteeing a fixed payout, 401(k)s place investment decision responsibility on the employee, influencing the account's growth.

2023 Retirement Contribution Limits: In 2023, individuals can contribute up to $22,500 to 401(k)s and $6,500 to IRAs, with higher limits in 2024. Additional catch-up contributions are available for those aged 50 or older. Over-contributing to a 401(k) necessitates withdrawing the excess funds, often accompanied by a 10% early withdrawal penalty by the IRS. Contributing at least enough to maximize an employer's 401(k) match is generally advisable. This ensures full utilization of the employer's contribution, doubling the retirement investment to the match limit.

In summary, retirement contributions are vital to transitioning into retirement while maintaining financial stability. Understanding the tax implications and strategic choices between pretax and after-tax contributions is crucial for maximizing long-term financial health and minimizing tax liability.

Tax Breaks: Definition, Types, and How to Access Them

A tax break is a benefit the government provides to reduce your overall tax liability. Tax breaks are available through various means, such as credits, deductions, exemptions, and income exclusions. These benefits are rooted in tax laws that strengthen the economy or support specific policy objectives. Certain groups, like religious organizations, often receive tax exemptions, while those affected by natural disasters can receive tax relief through extensions and waivers. Tax breaks offered to individuals and corporations significantly reduce tax liabilities through credits, deductions, exemptions, and exclusions. Some tax breaks do not require specific action (like life insurance proceeds, which are generally excluded from taxable income). In contrast, others must be claimed on tax returns and meet eligibility criteria.

Economic and Social Role of Tax Breaks: Tax breaks play a vital role in stimulating economic activity by increasing disposable income for taxpayers and investment capacity for businesses. They also encourage behaviors beneficial to society, like environmental consciousness. The implementation of tax breaks follows the enactment of state and federal tax laws, such as the Tax Cuts and Jobs Act (TCJA), signed in 2017.

Types of Tax Breaks

Tax Credits: A tax credit directly reduces your tax liability on a dollar-for-dollar basis. For instance, a $1,100 tax credit lowers your bill from $3,000 to $1,900. Credits have a more significant impact than deductions, directly reducing the tax amount owed.

Tax Deductions: Deductions decrease your gross income, reducing the income subject to taxes. The value of a deduction depends on your tax bracket. For example, in a 22% tax bracket, a $1,000 deduction saves you $220 in taxes. Depending on which option provides more significant financial benefits, taxpayers can choose between standard and itemizing deductions.

It would help if you generally claimed tax breaks on your income tax return to benefit from them. It is essential to stay informed about the various tax breaks available and understand which ones you are eligible for. Strategic use of tax breaks can lead to significant savings, effectively lowering your tax bill and increasing your refund. Tax breaks are crucial tools for reducing tax liabilities for individual taxpayers or businesses. Understanding the types of tax breaks available and how to access them can lead to substantial financial advantages. Consulting with a tax professional can further help in maximizing these benefits.

Understanding Tax Exclusions, Credits, Deductions, and Eligibility

Tax exclusions allow certain types of income or portions of income to be exempt from taxation. For example, child support payments, life insurance proceeds, and municipal bond income are typically not considered taxable income. Employer-paid health insurance premiums are exempt from federal income and payroll taxes, and the premiums paid by employees are usually not taxed. A notable tax exclusion applies to home sales. If you sell your main home and make a profit, you can exclude up to $250,000 of this gain from your taxable income (or up to $500,000 for married couples filing jointly). To qualify, you must have owned and lived in the home for at least two of the past five years and not have excluded gain from another home sale in the past two years. For those working abroad, the foreign-earned income exclusion allows individuals to exclude a certain amount from their income for tax purposes. The limits are $112,000 for the 2022 tax year and $120,000 for the 2023 tax year.

Tax credits and deductions aim to reduce your tax burden, but they operate differently. Tax credits directly decrease the tax you owe, dollar for dollar. For instance, a $1,000 tax credit reduces your tax bill by $1,000. In contrast, tax deductions reduce your taxable income. A $1,000 deduction in the 22% tax bracket would lower your tax bill by $220 because it reduces your taxable income by $1,000. Tax credits can often be more advantageous than deductions, especially if they are refundable. Refundable tax credits can reduce your tax liability to below zero, resulting in a refund. Deductions only decrease the amount of your taxable income and don't lead to a refund on their own. For instance, the annual gift exclusion was $16,000, increasing to $17,000 in 2023. This means you can give up these amounts to as many people as you want each year without affecting your lifetime gift and estate tax exemption. Generally, many tax breaks favor lower-income individuals, with deductions and credits often phasing out as income rises. Also, specific tax breaks target certain economic activities, like incentives for contributing to retirement accounts. By engaging in these activities, you can qualify for these tax benefits.

Using tax breaks aims to minimize your tax liability to the federal government. Both individuals and corporations can benefit from tax exclusions, deductions, and credits to reduce their taxable income or directly reduce the taxes owed. Taking advantage of these tax breaks is generally advisable to limit your exposure.

Maximizing Tax Savings To reduce your taxable income or increase your refund, consider whether you are eligible for tax deductions and credits and whether itemizing deductions is more beneficial than taking the standard deduction. Tax credits reduce tax liability directly, while deductions lower the taxable income. If itemized deductions exceed the standard deduction, itemizing could result in lower taxable income.

Review Questions

1. What distinguishes tax planning from tax compliance, and why is it essential for individuals and businesses?
2. How do tax planning principles contribute to efficient tax management and financial stability?
3. Identify the critical types of taxes in the UK and discuss their implications for individual and business finances.
4. Why is the timing of tax planning decisions critical, and what are the pivotal periods for tax planning actions?
5. Discuss the benefits of tax planning regarding financial flexibility and long-term savings. Provide examples of effective tax planning strategies.
6. How does consulting with a tax professional or advisor enhance the tax planning process and outcomes for taxpayers?

Discussion Points

1. The Role of Tax Planning in Financial Management: Explore the impact of strategic tax planning on personal and business financial health, including how it can lead to significant tax savings and contribute to achieving financial goals.
2. Challenges and Opportunities in Tax Planning: Discuss the challenges taxpayers face due to the complexity of tax laws and the opportunities that arise from being proactive and knowledgeable about tax planning strategies.
3. Future Trends in Tax Planning: Consider the potential changes in tax legislation and how taxpayers can adapt their tax planning strategies to remain efficient and compliant in a dynamic tax environment.

CHAPTER SIX: OPTIMIZING FINANCIAL HEALTH THROUGH TAX DEDUCTIONS, CREDITS, AND STRATEGIC PLANNING

Summary of Key Points

1. Tax Credits as a Direct Benefit: Tax credits, including refundable, nonrefundable, and partially refundable types, directly reduce tax liability and can significantly impact the amount of tax owed or refunded. Examples like the Earned Income Tax Credit (EITC) and American Opportunity Tax Credit (AOTC) substantially benefit eligible taxpayers.

2. The Importance of Tax Deductions: Tax deductions lower taxable income, with the amount of savings depending on the taxpayer's marginal tax rate. Standard deductions include business expenses, charitable donations, and student loan interest, which can lead to considerable tax savings when correctly claimed.

3. Tax Exclusions as a Form of Income Shielding: Certain types of income, such as life insurance proceeds or gains from home sales, can be excluded from taxation, offering another avenue for tax savings and financial optimization.

4. Navigating Federal and State Tax Credits: Both federal and state governments offer various tax credits to encourage specific behaviors and investments, such as installing solar panels or providing child and dependent care, which can lead to direct tax savings.

5. Strategies for Maximizing Tax Benefits: A strategic approach to tax

planning involves evaluating all potential deductions and credits, understanding income exclusions, and making informed decisions based on individual financial situations to minimize tax liability or maximize refunds.

6. Child Tax Credit and Family-Focused Tax Benefits: Recent changes and adjustments to tax credits for families, including the Child Tax Credit and Child and Dependent Care Tax Credit (CDCTC), highlight the dynamic nature of tax laws and the need for ongoing awareness and planning.

Maximizing Tax Benefits with Tax Deductions and Tax Credits

Tax Credits directly reduce your tax liability on a dollar-for-dollar basis. If a tax credit is refundable, it can reduce your tax bill to zero, and you may receive a refund for any excess amount. For instance, with a $4,000 tax credit and a $3,000 tax liability, you pay no taxes and receive a $1,000 refund. Earned Income Tax Credit (EITC) is a refundable credit for low-income workers. The credit amount varies based on income, number of dependent children, and filing status. It is essential to meet specific criteria to be eligible. Tax credit can be refundable or nonrefundable. Nonrefundable tax credits reduce the tax owed to zero but do not offer refunds for any credit balance remaining. Examples include the Adoption Credit and the Lifetime Learning Credit. Nonrefundable credits are valid only in the year they are reported and cannot be carried forward. Refundable tax credits are paid out fully. If a refundable tax credit reduces the tax liability below zero, the taxpayer receives a refund for the remaining amount. The Earned Income Tax Credit (EITC) is a crucial example. Partially refundable tax credits offer a partial refund. The American Opportunity Tax Credit (AOTC) for education is an example, offering a partial refund if the credit reduces the tax liability below zero.

Federal and State Tax Credits: Tax credits are provided by federal and state governments to encourage behaviors beneficial to the economy, environment, or specific policy goals. Common tax credits include solar panel installation, child and dependent care, education, and adoption.

Deductions reduce your taxable income. The tax savings from a deduction depend on your marginal tax rate. For example, if your marginal tax rate is 22 percent, a $1,000 deduction saves you $220 in taxes. Tax deductions lower your taxable income and, consequently, your tax liability. Examples include certain business expenses, student loan interest, and capital losses. Research and understanding lesser-known deductions can significantly impact your tax savings. Specific examples of tax deductions are described below:

1. Business Travel Expenses: Self-employed individuals can deduct travel expenses related to their business. Employees may exclude employer reimbursements for business travel from their income.
2. Charitable Donations: Contributions to qualified charitable organizations can be deductible. Although the $300 deduction for single filers without itemizing is no longer available after 2021, you can still claim charitable donations if you itemize deductions.
3. Student Loan Interest: You can deduct interest on student loans. If parents pay the interest on loans in your name, you can still claim this deduction if you are not a dependent.
4. Tax Exclusions: Exclusions allow certain types of income exempt from taxation, such as life insurance proceeds or income from municipal bonds. For instance, home sale gains of up to $250,000 ($500,000 for married couples) can be excluded under certain conditions. Foreign-earned income also has an exclusion limit.

Strategic Approach to Tax Planning

To minimize your tax liability or maximize refunds, consider all available deductions and credits:

1. Evaluate Deductions: Assess if itemizing deductions could be more beneficial than taking the standard deduction.
2. Identify Credits: Determine if you qualify for any tax credits that can reduce your tax bill or even provide a refund.
3. Understand Exclusions: Be aware of income types that can be excluded

from taxation and plan accordingly.

Navigating tax deductions, credits, and exclusions can be complex but rewarding. Understanding these tax-saving mechanisms and how they apply to your situation is crucial for effective tax planning. Consult a tax professional, if needed, to ensure you leverage these options to their fullest potential and comply with tax laws.

Child Tax Credit Adjustments and Tax Credits for Families

Child Tax Credit - Recent Changes: The American Rescue Plan Act (ARPA) temporarily enhanced the Child Tax Credit for 2021, increasing the amount and making it fully refundable, with advance payments to taxpayers. However, these changes expired at the end of 2021. For 2022 and 2023, the Child Tax Credit has reverted to $2,000 per qualifying child under 17, with the maximum refundable portion being $1,600 in 2023, up from $1,500 in 2022. Any future changes to this credit would require new legislation. The American Rescue Plan introduced several changes, including stimulus checks and adjustments to the Child Tax Credit and EITC. These changes were temporary and primarily applied to the 2021 tax year.

Child and Dependent Care Tax Credit (CDCTC): The CDCTC assists with expenses for the care of children under age 12, disabled spouses, or other dependents, enabling the taxpayer to work or look for work. The credit's value is a percentage of the taxpayer's earned income and is reduced for those with higher adjusted gross incomes (AGIs), phasing out entirely at an AGI of $438,000. For 2021, the CDCTC's rate increased for lower-income workers but decreased for higher-income earners. These enhancements were only for one year, so unless extended, the CDCTC for 2022 and 2023 will revert to its previous structure.

Adoption Credit or Exclusion: Taxpayers adopting a child under 18 or a disabled person can claim tax benefits for qualified adoption expenses, with a maximum credit of $15,950 per child in 2023. Employer-provided benefits for adoption can also be excluded from taxable income up to the same amount.

Benefits above this limit are taxable.

Tax Credits for Education Expenses

Lifetime Learning Credit: Available for qualified postsecondary educational expenses, the credit has income phase-out thresholds ($80,000 for single filers, $160,000 for joint filers in 2023). The credit amount is reduced for higher incomes, with a maximum credit of $2,000.

American Opportunity Tax Credit: A maximum annual credit of $2,500 per eligible student is offered. The student must be enrolled at least half-time in a degree program. The credit is partially refundable, and income phase-outs apply ($80,000 for singles and $160,000 for joint filers).

Itemizing Tax Deductions

Considering their specific financial situations and expenses, taxpayers should evaluate whether itemizing deductions is more beneficial than taking the standard deduction. Deductible expenses include substantial unreimbursed medical expenses, home mortgage interest, casualty or theft losses, and charitable contributions. The standard deduction amounts for 2022 and 2023 vary based on filing status.

Filing Considerations and Eligibility for Multiple Credits

Taxpayers can claim multiple credits like the EITC, Child Tax Credit, and CDCTC if they meet the qualifications. It is possible to claim deductions like student loan interest without itemizing deductions. Certain tax credits and deductions have phase-out thresholds based on income, affecting their value or eligibility.

In summary, tax laws and credits can be complex and subject to change. It is advisable to stay informed about tax regulations and consult with a tax professional for personalized guidance to maximize potential tax benefits. The IRS website also offers extensive resources for understanding tax credits, deductions, and filing requirements.

Business Expenses and Tax Implications

Business expenses are costs incurred during the normal operations of a business. They are essential for businesses of all sizes and types, playing a crucial role in financial and tax reporting. These expenses are tracked throughout the year for tax purposes, and they are subtracted from a business's revenue to calculate its taxable net income. Business expenses are broadly categorized into capital expenditures (long-term investments in the business) and operational expenditures (day-to-day operational costs). Business expenses, or deductions, are subtracted from a business's revenue to determine its taxable income.

The IRS allows businesses to deduct expenses deemed "ordinary and necessary" for the business's industry. This means the expenses are ordinary and appropriate for the business type.

Eligibility for Deduction: Some business expenses are entirely deductible, including advertising costs, employee training, legal fees, office supplies, and utility expenses. Certain expenses may only be partially deductible based on IRS guidelines.

Reporting on Expenses

Businesses use the income statement to report expenses, typically categorized into direct costs, indirect costs, and interest expenses.

1. Direct Costs include the cost of goods sold (COGS), reflecting expenses directly associated with producing goods or services.
2. Indirect Costs: Expenses like executive compensation, marketing, and general expenses are subtracted from gross profit to calculate operating profit.
3. Depreciation: This indirect expense involves expensing business assets such as equipment and property over several years.

Special Expense Categories

1. Gifts, Meals, and Entertainment: The IRS limits deductions for these expenses, with specific rules for what percentage can be deducted.
2. Interest Expenses: Interest is deducted last on the income statement to arrive at taxable income.

Personal vs. Business Expenses

Only the business portion is deductible when expenses serve personal and business purposes. This applies to expenses like vehicle use and home office costs. Certain expenses, including bribes, lobbying costs, penalties, fines, and political contributions, are not deductible for business purposes.

Key IRS Definitions

1. 'Ordinary and Necessary' Business Expense: A deductible expense that is common and appropriate in the industry, though not necessarily essential.
2. Non-deductible business expenses: Expenses with a personal benefit or unrelated to business activities.

Specific Deductions

1. Vehicle Use: If a vehicle is used for both personal and business purposes, only the business-related costs are deductible.
2. Home Office: Expenses related to a home office used exclusively for business can be deducted.

For effective tax management, businesses must accurately report "ordinary and necessary" expenses. Understanding which expenses are fully or partially deductible is crucial for calculating accurate taxable income and ensuring compliance with IRS regulations.

Business Use of Home: Portions of a home used exclusively for business may be deductible. Deductions are based on the percentage of the home used for business.

Amortization vs. Depreciation: Amortization is used for intangible assets like patents or trademarks, typically using the straight-line method over the asset's useful life. Intangible assets usually have no salvage value. Depreciation applies to tangible assets like vehicles or equipment, reflecting their wear and tear over time. There are various depreciation methods.

Understanding Depreciation in Business

Depreciation is expensing a fixed asset's cost over its expected useful life. It applies to tangible assets (physical objects) such as buildings, machinery, equipment, vehicles, and office furniture, involving subtracting the asset's salvage (residual) value from its original cost. The resulting amount is spread evenly across the asset's useful life as annual depreciation expenses. Each year's depreciation amount can be used as a tax deduction until the asset's useful life ends.

Example of Depreciation: Consider a company that purchases an office building. The building was used for many years before the company moved to a new location. Even if the original building is somewhat worn, it retains some value. Its initial cost, minus any potential resale value, is distributed across its expected lifespan, with a portion recognized annually as an expense.

Depreciation Methods

1. Straight-Line Method: The asset's cost is evenly depreciated over its useful life.
2. Declining Balance: Accelerated depreciation in the asset's early years, using a fixed rate applied to its current book value.
3. Double Declining Balance Method: An accelerated method that doubles the straight-line rate and applies it to the current book value.
4. Sum-of-the-Years' Digits Method: A declining fraction (based on the

sum of the years' digits) is applied yearly to the asset's depreciable base.

5. Units of Production: Depreciation based on actual usage (e.g., vehicle mileage).

Depreciation reflects a decrease in an asset's value over time, whereas amortization spreads an asset's cost over its lifespan. Amortization typically uses the straight-line method, while depreciation offers multiple methods. Depreciation can be accelerated, whereas amortization usually involves consistent annual charges. Depreciation considers salvage value in calculations, whereas amortization does not. Depreciation entries posted to accumulated depreciation are contra-asset accounts. Amortization may not always use contra accounts.

Example from Amazon's 2021 Annual Report: Amazon reported a combined $34.3 billion in depreciation and amortization. Amazon had $238.8 billion in gross property and equipment, with $78.5 billion in accumulated depreciation and amortization, indicating that a significant portion of its assets had been depreciated. The net property and equipment value were reported at $160.3 billion. Amazon classified intangible assets as either finite-lived or in-process for research and development. Most were marketing-related or contract-based, totaling nearly $7 billion, with $1.8 billion in accumulated amortization.

Understanding Depreciation and Amortization: Both depreciation and amortization are accounting techniques to allocate the cost of assets over time. While they serve a similar purpose, the key distinctions lie in the types of assets they apply to and the methods used for calculation. Understanding these concepts is crucial for accurately reporting financial statements and making informed business decisions.

Depletion in Business Assets

Depletion is an accounting method primarily for natural resources like oil wells. It allows a business to allocate the setup costs of a resource over its expected life. The different treatments of depletion are explained below:

1. Percentage Depletion: Assigns a fixed percentage of gross income from resource extraction as a deduction.
2. Cost Depletion: Considers the property's basis, total recoverable reserves, and the quantity of resources sold.

Depreciation, amortization, and depletion are expenses recognized without immediate cash outflows. These are treated as non-cash transactions, essential for planning and managing capital expenditures. Land cannot be depreciated, as it does not diminish in value over time, according to the IRS.

Examples

Amortization: A company amortizing a 10-year patent recognizes 10% of its cost annually, reducing its carrying value each year.

Depreciation: Using the sum-of-the-years digits method, a vehicle's depreciation is higher in the initial years, reflecting its higher efficiency and usage.

R&D Tax Credits and Deductions

These deductions aim to encourage U.S. businesses to invest in research. They come in the form of immediate deduction of R&D expenditures (I.R.C. §174) and credit for increased research expenditures (I.R.C. §41).

Changes and Qualifications

1. TCJA Impact: The corporate tax rate reduction in the TCJA increased the research credit benefit. However, starting in 2022, R&D costs must be amortized over five years (or 15 years for foreign research).
2. Qualifying Research: Must meet specific criteria, including technological nature, aim to develop new business components, and involve a process of experimentation.
3. Eligibility: Determined by the nature of business activities and involve-

ment in technological advancements.

Utilizing R&D Tax Credits: A limitation is that no double benefit for the same expenditure is allowed under I.R.C. §280C. Tax planning involves analyzing R&D expenditures, possible credits, and amortization to optimize tax benefits. Understanding the nuances of depletion, depreciation, amortization, and R&D tax credits is crucial in business taxation. Each has specific applications and impacts on a company's financial and tax planning. Applying these methods and understanding tax incentives, especially in research and development, can significantly benefit a company's financial health and innovation capabilities.

Understanding Renewable Energy Credits (RECs) and Their Impact

Renewable Energy Credits, commonly known as RECs, are market-based instruments that provide evidence of electricity generation from renewable energy sources. Each REC certifies the generation of one megawatt-hour (MWh) of electricity from renewable resources such as wind, solar, or hydroelectric power, which is then fed into the general power grid. RECs act as a tracking mechanism for renewable energy generation. When a company purchases RECs, it essentially buys proof that some of its electricity consumption is sourced from renewable energy. This system allows businesses to support green energy initiatives, even if they cannot generate renewable energy onsite.
   Purchasing RECs can be beneficial if your business aims to:

1. Support renewable energy development.
2. Face obstacles in directly implementing renewable energy solutions.
3. Desire to reduce carbon footprint and energy usage.
4. Have significant environmental objectives to meet.

RECs are generated when a renewable energy facility, like a solar farm or wind turbine, produces and supplies 1 MWh of electricity to the grid. Each unit of energy produced translates into a REC, which the facility can retain or sell.

Benefits of RECs

1. Proof of Renewable Energy Use: RECs offer evidence that your business supports and uses renewable energy.
2. Cost-Effective: They provide an alternative to costly investments in renewable energy infrastructure.
3. Emission Reduction: RECs aid in reducing overall carbon emissions and promote environmental sustainability.
4. Market Demand: Buying RECs increases demand for renewable energy, encouraging more production and potentially lowering costs.

RECs are ideal for:

1. Environmentally conscious businesses.
2. Companies that are unable to implement onsite renewable energy projects.
3. Businesses aiming to reduce their environmental impact and meet sustainability goals.
4. Regulatory Aspect: Some states mandate that utilities meet Renewable Portfolio Standards (RPS), requiring a specific percentage of energy from renewable sources. Utilities, in turn, use RECs to comply with these regulations.

The process of buying RECs can be intricate. Energy consultancy firms like EnergyWatch assist in understanding the market, ensuring that renewable energy procurement aligns with operational goals and monitoring contract performance. With increasing focus on net-zero emissions, RECs are gaining prominence. However, tracking renewable energy production can be challenging due to diverse data sources. Advanced software solutions like WatchWire can simplify monitoring and reporting renewable energy performance.

Energy Expense Management: Energy is a significant yet manageable operational expense. Effective real-time and interval data monitoring can provide better control and understanding of energy costs. During the festive season, it is vital to remember the environmental impact of increased energy use and consider integrating RECs or other sustainable practices into holiday planning.

In summary, RECs play a crucial role in supporting renewable energy, offering a practical solution for businesses to contribute to environmental sustainability. Understanding and effectively managing REC purchases can significantly impact a company's energy strategy and carbon footprint.

Review Questions

1. What distinguishes refundable, nonrefundable, and partially refundable tax credits, and how do they impact a taxpayer's financial situation?
2. How do tax deductions work, and what standard deductions can lower taxpayers' taxable income?
3. What are tax exclusions, and how do they differ from deductions and credits regarding reducing tax liability?
4. Describe the role of federal and state tax credits in encouraging specific economic and social behaviors among taxpayers.
5. How can taxpayers strategically approach tax planning to maximize potential benefits?
6. Discuss the significance of recent changes to the Child Tax Credit and how they affect family tax planning.

Discussion Points

1. Evaluating the Impact of Tax Legislation Changes: Consider how recent and potential changes to tax legislation, particularly regarding tax credits and deductions, can affect taxpayers' strategies for minimizing tax liabilities and maximizing refunds.
2. The Role of Tax Professionals in Strategic Tax Planning: Discuss the importance of consulting with tax professionals for personalized guidance on navigating complex tax laws and optimizing tax benefits, especially with frequently changing tax codes and regulations.

3. Balancing Between Short-term Benefits and Long-term Tax Planning: Explore the challenges and strategies for balancing immediate tax savings through credits and deductions with long-term financial planning goals, including retirement savings and investments.

CHAPTER SEVEN: STRATEGIC TAX PLANNING AND COMPLIANCE

Summary of Key Points

1. Role of Internal Audit and Tax Compliance: The Internal Audit function at the University of San Francisco ensures the efficiency and effectiveness of operations through independent assurance and consulting services. This includes enhancing risk management, internal controls, and governance processes to achieve strategic objectives.

2. Comprehensive Tax Function Responsibilities: The university's tax function is crucial in complying with various tax laws and regulations, including payroll, property, sales, and use taxes. It also plays a crucial role in preparing tax filings, training staff, and coordinating with external tax audits.

3. Importance of Effective Tax Risk Management: In a complex tax environment, managing tax risks is essential to avoid penalties, reputational damage, and legal issues. Effective risk management strategies are vital for long-term financial stability and compliance.

4. Strategies for Tax Risk Management: Developing a comprehensive tax risk management plan involves identifying potential risks, prioritizing them, developing mitigation strategies, and continuously monitoring and updating the plan. This includes training the tax team and utilizing technology for better compliance and risk control.

Internal Audit and Tax Compliance – The Case of the University of San Francisco

The University of San Francisco's Internal Audit function is pivotal in enhancing the efficiency and effectiveness of the university's operations. The internal audit team operates independently and objectively and provides crucial assurance and consulting services. These services aim to improve the university's risk management, internal control systems, and governance processes. The overarching goal is to support the university in achieving its strategic objectives, adhering to core values, and realizing its vision and mission.

The university's tax function ensures compliance with various federal, state, and local tax laws and regulations. This broad spectrum covers payroll taxes, nonresident alien taxes, sales and use taxes, unrelated business income taxes, property taxes, excise taxes, hotel taxes, and more. The tax team also handles the preparation of corresponding information returns and filings. An essential part of their role includes aiding departments with tax compliance issues, providing necessary staff training, and coordinating external tax audits and reviews. Departments contacted by external auditors are advised to inform the Associate Vice President of Tax Compliance and Internal Audit.

In the current complex tax environment, managing tax risks is increasingly vital for businesses of various sizes and sectors. Addressing tax risks effectively is critical to avoiding penalties, reputational damage, and legal issues and ensuring financial stability and operational success. Implementing a robust risk management strategy is essential for navigating the complexities of taxation.

Risk Management in Tax

Risk management involves identifying, assessing, prioritizing, and mitigating potential threats or uncertainties. This process is crucial for a sustainable business model. Tax risk management is critical due to the constant changes in indirect tax laws and regulations across jurisdictions. Ineffective management of tax risks can lead to penalties, fines, and overall instability. The benefits of risk management are further elaborated below:

1. Long-term Financial Stability: Efficient management of indirect taxes is crucial to avoid unexpected financial burdens and impacts on profitability.
2. Tax Compliance and Penalty Avoidance: Tax compliance, especially in complex industries, is essential to minimize the risk of penalties and additional charges.
3. Maintaining a Trusted Brand Reputation: Consistent compliance enhances trust in your brand, which is especially important in industries like vapor, where license loss can have significant implications.
4. Competitive Advantage: Effective tax risk management positions businesses better in the market, allowing for growth and adaptation without unexpected tax liabilities.

Common Tax Risks in the Excise Tax Industry

1. Assessments: Discrepancies found by the state leading to potential audits.
2. Audit Risks: Resulting from errors or anomalies in tax documents.
3. Legislative Changes: Frequent changes in tax legislation require agility and adjustments in compliance procedures.
4. Filing Errors: This can lead to financial losses and trigger audits.
5. Incorrect Registration: This can lead to extended audit periods.
6. Late Filings: Risk incurring penalties and interest.
7. Overpayments: Result in financial losses that require refund requests.
8. Tax Controversy: Disputes between the business and taxing jurisdiction, often requiring legal intervention.

The University of San Francisco's commitment to internal audit and tax compliance is integral to its operational integrity. In the broader context, understanding and managing tax risks, particularly in indirect taxation, is crucial for any business aiming to maintain financial stability and a strong reputation in an ever-changing tax landscape.

Effective Tax Risk Management Strategies

Developing a Comprehensive Tax Risk Management Plan Creating a thorough tax risk management plan is crucial for any organization. Here are essential steps to consider:

1. Identify Risks: Determine existing and potential tax risks.
2. Triage Risks: Prioritize the identified risks based on impact.
3. Develop Mitigation Strategies: Formulate strategies to minimize or eliminate risks.
4. Train the Team: Educate the tax team on the identified strategies.
5. Monitor and Update: Regularly review and refine the plan to address new risks.

A well-crafted plan enhances transparency and accountability and ensures all team members understand their role in managing tax risks.

Three Lines of Defense Model

1. First Line - Frontline Tax Team: Handles daily risk management and preventive measures.
2. Second Line - Tax Director/Manager: Provides oversight, policy enforcement, and guidance.
3. Third Line - Internal Audit: Evaluate and improve the effectiveness of the first two lines.

This model promotes risk awareness and fosters a culture of proactive risk management across the organization, encouraging collaboration between the tax team and other departments such as finance and legal. This synergy helps in identifying and mitigating cross-functional tax risks. A transparent and well-defined workflow enhances understanding and helps in anticipating potential risks. Other strengths of the model include:

Establishing a Risk-Aware Culture: Promote a culture where every process and transaction is "audit ready." This approach prevents cutting corners and instills habits safeguarding the company against potential risks.

1. Monitoring and Controlling Risks: Utilize dynamic tax compliance software and reconciliation technology to monitor and identify tax record discrepancies. Regular internal audits and reporting are crucial for ensuring accurate tax liabilities.
2. Staying Informed on Industry Changes: Stay updated with the latest tax laws and regulations changes through continuous education and networking with industry peers. This knowledge is vital in adapting to the dynamic tax environment.
3. Encouraging Executive Team Involvement in Tax Risk Management
4. Educate the Executive Team: Inform them about the impacts of tax issues on the organization's risk profile and financial performance.
5. Align Tax and Business Objectives: Demonstrate how tax planning aligns with the company's objectives.
6. Develop and Share Risk Assessments: Present tax-related risks in an accessible format, using visual tools for better understanding.
7. Scenario Analysis: Conduct analyses to show the impact of various tax strategies or law changes on the organization.

Leveraging Technology in Tax Administration

1. Identifying the Tax Base: Use technology to identify and broaden the tax base.
2. Monitoring Compliance: Implement tools to monitor taxpayer compliance efficiently.
3. Facilitating Compliance: Simplify tax compliance through user-friendly technologies.
4. Addressing Challenges: Ensure basic infrastructure and internet connec-

tivity, manage taxpayer and collector resistance, and create a supportive regulatory environment for technology adoption.

Effective tax risk management is integral to an organization's financial stability and compliance. By implementing structured risk management plans, promoting a culture of risk awareness, and utilizing modern technology, organizations can navigate the complex world of taxation more effectively and efficiently.

Optimizing Tax Strategies through Technology and Planning

Technology significantly enhances three core functions of tax administrations:

1. Identifying the Tax Base: Technology aids in accurately identifying tax compliance for businesses and individuals. By digitizing taxpayer registration and using third-party information, authorities can better understand taxable entities and their activities, leading to more comprehensive tax databases. Electronic fiscal devices (EFDs) and digital payment tracking further accurately determine taxes due.
2. Monitoring Compliance: Advanced data analytics enable tax authorities to automate and cross-verify self-reported tax liabilities against other data sources. This approach improves transparency and efficiency in auditing processes, focusing on risk-based audits.
3. Facilitating Compliance: Technological tools like EFDs, e-filing, and e-payment systems enhance the taxpayer experience by simplifying interactions with tax authorities. This not only reduces compliance costs but also minimizes opportunities for corrupt practices.

Addressing Technology Limitations in Taxation

1. Infrastructure: Inadequate infrastructure, such as unstable internet connectivity, can hinder effective tax technology deployment. Tax authorities can cater to less connected populations by offering more straightforward, offline solutions.
2. The Human Factor: Resistance from taxpayers and tax officials due to various reasons, including cost and change aversion, can impede technology adoption. Tailored training and change management strategies can address these challenges.
3. Institutional Strategy: Success in technology adoption requires strong leadership buy-in, strategic planning, and appropriate sequencing of technological upgrades.
4. Regulatory Framework: Data privacy and confidentiality concerns can restrict data sharing. Creating a centralized, automated platform accessible by relevant institutions can facilitate efficient taxpayer identification and information cross-checking.

Strategic Tax Planning Examples

1. Tax Diversification: Balancing contributions between traditional tax-deferred and Roth accounts can provide flexibility and tax efficiency in retirement.
2. Tax Gain/Loss Harvesting: Strategic selling of assets to realize capital gains or losses can optimize tax outcomes.
3. Social Security Taxation: Understanding how different income sources affect the taxation of Social Security benefits is crucial for retirement planning.
4. Charitable Giving Strategies: Utilizing Qualified Charitable Distributions (QCDs) and Donor-Advised Funds can offer tax advantages while supporting philanthropic goals.
5. Multi-Year Tax Planning: Developing a long-term tax strategy can significantly impact retirement and generational wealth transfer financial

outcomes.

Incorporating Tax into Risk Management Strategy

1. Educate Executive Team: Raise awareness among executives about the impact of tax-related issues on organizational risk.
2. Align Tax with Business Goals: Demonstrate how tax strategies support broader business objectives.
3. Risk Assessment and Reporting: Develop structured risk assessments and present findings in an executive-friendly format.
4. Continuous Learning: Stay informed about industry changes and engage with peers and experts to navigate the dynamic tax landscape.

Leveraging technology in tax administration and adopting comprehensive tax planning strategies are essential for effective tax risk management. These approaches ensure compliance and enhance operational efficiency and financial stability. Engaging leadership and fostering a culture that values proactive tax planning can position organizations to navigate tax complexities better and optimize financial outcomes.

Maximizing Financial Opportunities Through Strategic Tax Planning and Global Compliance

Effective tax planning is crucial for minimizing tax liabilities and ensuring you and your family achieve your desired retirement lifestyle. Tax planning can be a powerful tool in shaping your financial independence. Consider using advanced financial planning tools to explore how tax planning can enhance your retirement plans. These tools, often used by Certified Financial Planner™ professionals, can include sections for reviewing your tax situation, enabling you to start crafting a multi-year tax strategy from the comfort of your home. For further guidance on these tax planning strategies or using financial planning tools, consider reaching out to financial experts. Many offer virtual and in-person consultations to discuss how these strategies can benefit you. In

April 2019, at the 19th Annual US and Europe Tax Practice Trends Conference in Paris, several global tax trends were highlighted, emphasizing the importance of compliance for businesses operating internationally. Understanding and adapting to these trends is crucial for businesses worldwide.

The Rise of Digital Tax Reporting: Digitalization in tax reporting demands that businesses provide detailed information to tax authorities in a new format. This transition may require significant investments in technology and personnel. Despite the challenges, digital tax reporting also presents opportunities for improved taxpayer services, as seen in Spain's virtual international tax system and Australia's 'Alex, your Virtual Assistant.'

Tax Rate and Rule Changes: Changes in Europe's VAT system and US tax reforms are influencing global business structures. It is essential for companies, especially those engaged in online trading, to stay informed and adapt to these changes.

Tax Transparency: Implementing Transfer Pricing (TP) and Country-by-Country Reporting (CbCR) requirements marks a move toward greater tax transparency. Businesses must now adhere to these new reporting standards, with an increasing number of countries outside Europe adopting OECD guidelines.

Growth in Business Incentives: Despite efforts to level the playing field in corporate tax, governments continue to offer incentives to attract foreign investment. Notably, R&D tax incentives are becoming more prevalent, with many EU countries offering tax benefits for R&D activities.

Global Compliance and Tax Management Solutions

Businesses worldwide are affected by these evolving tax trends and must take necessary steps for compliance. Engaging with global accounting and tax experts can provide invaluable support in navigating these changes. Services offered can include:

1. Assessing the impact of impending tax changes on your business.
2. Managing tax reporting using compliant tools and systems.

3. Providing transitional accounting and tax compliance solutions during system updates.

Strategic tax planning and adapting to global tax trends are essential for individual financial success and business compliance. Whether planning for retirement or operating a business internationally, staying informed and seeking expert advice can significantly enhance financial outcomes and ensure compliance in a rapidly changing tax landscape.

Review Questions

1. What is the primary goal of the Internal Audit function at the University of San Francisco?
2. How does the university's tax function ensure compliance with various tax laws and regulations?
3. Why is tax risk management increasingly important for organizations in the current tax environment?
4. What are some key strategies for effective organizational tax risk management?

Discussion Points

1. Challenges in Tax Compliance and Risk Management: Discuss the challenges organizations face in staying compliant with changing tax laws and managing tax risks effectively, considering the diverse types of taxes and potential penalties for non-compliance.
2. The Role of Technology in Tax Administration: Explore how technology can aid in identifying the tax base, monitoring compliance, and facilitating compliance, as well as the limitations and challenges associated with technology implementation in tax administration.
3. Strategic Tax Planning for Long-term Financial Goals: Consider the importance of strategic tax planning in achieving financial stability and success for individuals planning for retirement and businesses aiming

for growth and compliance in a global tax landscape.

SOURCES

Fiscal Policy for Economic Development: An Overview Benedict Clements, Sanjeev Gupta, And Gabriela Inchauste https://www.imf.org/external/pubs/nft/2004/hcd/ch01.pdf

Chapter 23 - Environmental Taxation and Regulation A. Lans Bovenberg, Lawrence H. Goulder https://www.sciencedirect.com/science/article/abs/pii/S1573442002800271

Chapter 32 - What is a Sustainable Public Debt? P. D'Erasmo E.G. Mendoza J. Zhang https://www.sciencedirect.com/science/article/abs/pii/S1574004816000148

All About Fiscal Policy: What It Is, Why It Matters, and Examples https://www.investopedia.com/terms/f/fiscalpolicy.asp

"Fiscal Policy" Before Keynes' General Theory Marianne Johnson file:///C:/Users/USER/Downloads/SSRN-id3252526.pdf

Fiscal Policy: Taking and Giving Away Mark Horton, Asmaa El-Ganainy https://www.imf.org/en/Publications/fandd/issues/Series/Back-to-Basics/Fiscal-Policy

Expansionary and Contractionary Fiscal Policy https://courses.lumenlearning.com/wm-macroeconomics/chapter/expansionary-and-contractionary-fiscal-policy/

Expansionary Fiscal Policy: Risks and Examples https://www.investopedia.com/terms/e/expansionary_policy.asp

Monetary Policy vs. Fiscal Policy: What's the Difference? https://www.investopedia.com/ask/answers/100314/whats-difference-between-monetary-policy-and-fiscal-policy.asp

How fiscal policy impacts business https://gocardless.com/guides/posts/how-fiscal-policy-impacts-business/

Fiscal Policy: Economic Effects Jeffrey M. Stupak Analyst in Macroeconomic Policy file:///C:/Users/USER/Documents/20finance/2019054c4pdf

Tax and Fiscal Policy in Response to the Coronavirus Crisis: Strengthening Confidence and Resilience https://read.oecd-ilibrary.org/view/?ref=128_128575-06raktc0aa&title=Tax-and-Fiscal-Policy-in-Response-to-the-Coronavirus-Crisis

Fiscal policy and high inflation https://www.ecb.europa.eu/pub/economic-bulletin/articles/2023/html/ecb.ebart202302_01~2bd46eff8f.en.html

All About Fiscal Policy: What It Is, Why It Matters, and Examples ADAM HAYES https://www.investopedia.com/terms/f/fiscalpolicy.asp

A Monetary and Fiscal History of the United States, 1961-2022 Alan Blinder https://www.milkenreview.org/articles/a-monetary-and-fiscal-history-of-the-united-states-1961-2022

Interactions between fiscal and monetary policies: a brief history of a long relationship https://www.pse-journal.hr/en/archive/interactions-between-fiscal-and-monetary-policies-a-brief-history-of-a-long-relationship_7902/

Taxation https://www.britannica.com/money/topic/taxation

Chapter 2 Fundamental principles of taxation https://www.oecd-ilibrary.org/docserver/9789264218789-5-en.pdf?e=1703964323&id=id&accname=guest&checksum=91EDD7C1544E5D4777ECE5A320702571

The Theoretical Foundations of Regulation on Public Finances http://real.mtak.hu/146408/1/CEALSCEPhD02RegulationofPublicFinances2.pdf

Public Finance: Theory and Practice in the Central European Transition https://www.nispa.org/files/publications/ebooks/Public-Finance-Theory-and-Practice.pdf

What Are Public Goods? Definition, How They Work, and Example JASON FERNANDO https://www.investopedia.com/terms/p/public-good.asp

Public Goods https://courses.lumenlearning.com/wm-microeconomics/chapter/public-goods/

The rationale for public sector intervention in the economy https://www.lo

ndon.gov.uk/sites/default/files/gla_migrate_files_destination/rationale_
for_public_sector_intervention.pdf

Free Rider Benefiting from a common resource without paying for it
https://corporatefinanceinstitute.com/resources/economics/free-rider/

Free-rider problem https://en.wikipedia.org/wiki/Free-rider_problem#
:~:text=In%20the%20social%20sciences%2C%20the,goods%20of%20a%
20communal%20nature

The advantage of international fiscal cooperation under alternative monetary regimes https://www.sciencedirect.com/science/article/abs/pii/S01762
68096000122

Who benefits from international fiscal cooperation? The role of cross-
country asymmetries George Liontos a, Apostolis Philippopoulos https://ww
w.sciencedirect.com/science/article/abs/pii/S1703494923000026

International tax cooperation and capital mobility https://repositorio.cepa
l.org/server/api/core/bitstreams/e4d0935a-6ae8-4ba7-8430-c7601f8cb05
8/content

Case Studies of Fiscal Councils—Functions and Impact https://www.imf.or
g/external/np/pp/eng/2013/071613a.pdf

Chapter 7 Broader tax challenges raised by the digital economy https://w
ww.oecd-ilibrary.org/docserver/9789264218789-10-en.pdf?expires=17039
75653&id=id&accname=guest&checksum=410D401BCAC2A4DD84E56FC0E
D2A1892

Taxing the Digital Economy in Latin America and the Caribbean: What can
be done https://www.afronomicslaw.org/2020/12/09/taxing-the-digital-ec
onomy-in-latin-america-and-the-caribbean-what-can-be-done

Green Fiscal Reforms, Environment and Sustainable Development https://o
nlineacademicpress.com/index.php/IJAEFA/article/view/6/375

What Are Smart Contracts on the Blockchain and How They Work https://w
ww.investopedia.com/terms/s/smart-contracts.asp

Aging Populations and
Public Pension Schemes https://www.imf.org/external/pubs/nft/op/147/

Fiscal Policy David N. Weil https://www.econlib.org/library/Enc/FiscalPoli
cy.html

Do Enlarged Fiscal Deficits Cause Inflation: The Historical Record Michael D. Bordo Mickey D. Levy Working Paper 28195 https://www.nber.org/system/files/working_papers/w28195/w28195.pdf

Fiscal Policy Can Help Tame Inflation and Protect the Most Vulnerable https://www.imf.org/en/Blogs/Articles/2023/04/03/fiscal-policy-can-help-tame-inflation-and-protect-the-most-vulnerable

Public Policy Origins, Practice, and Analysis https://web.ung.edu/media/university-press/public-policy.pdf?t=1661449833017

What are the principles of good taxation? https://www.futurelearn.com/info/courses/public-financial-management/0/steps/14705#:~:text=The%20principles%20of%20good%20taxation%20were%20formulated%20many%20years%20ago,%2C%20certainty%2C%20convenience%20and%20efficiency

Principles of Taxation https://taxjustice-and-poverty.org/fileadmin/Datein/Taxjustice_and_Poverty/Introduction/05_Principles.pdf

Taxes Definition: Type, Who Pays and Why https://www.investopedia.com/terms/t/taxes.asp

Classes of taxes https://www.britannica.com/money/topic/taxation/Classes-of-taxes

Analysis of Assessment Methods of Tax Burden: Theoretical Aspect file:///C:/Users/USER/Downloads/2089-Article%20Text-6378-1-10-20120807.pdf

Tax shift https://en.wikipedia.org/wiki/Tax_shift#:~:text=Tax%20shift%20is%20a%20kind,the%20redistribution%20of%20tax%20burden

Distributional effects https://en.wikipedia.org/wiki/Distributional_effects#:~:text=A%20distributional%20effect%20is%20the,cost%20allocations%20of%20a%20project

Government Spending https://corporatefinanceinstitute.com/resources/economics/government-spending/

Government spending https://en.wikipedia.org/wiki/Government_spending

What Are Some Examples of Debt Instruments? https://www.investopedia.com/ask/answers/050515/what-are-some-examples-debt-instruments.asp

What Is a Debt Instrument? Definition, Structure, and Types https://www.investopedia.com/terms/d/debtinstrument.asp

Government Debt Management: Designing Debt Management Strategies https://thedocs.worldbank.org/en/doc/194071527797532524-0340022018/original/GDM1backgroundnotes.pdf

How to design a stimulus package https://cepr.org/voxeu/columns/how-design-stimulus-package

Green stimulus after the 2008 crisis: Learning from successes and failures https://www.iea.org/articles/green-stimulus-after-the-2008-crisis

A Comparison of Selected Stimulus Packages in 2008 and 2020: investing in Renewable Energy, Sustainable Agriculture and Food Security, and Gender Equality and the Empowerment of Women for Structural Economic transformation https://unctad.org/system/files/information-document/osg_2020-12-18_StimulusPackages_en.pdf

The United States' Response to COVID-19: A Case Study of the First Year https://globalhealthsciences.ucsf.edu/sites/globalhealthsciences.ucsf.edu/files/covid-us-case-study.pdf

China's Policy Experience in Responding to Covid-19 Shock https://unctad.org/system/files/official-document/BRI-Project_RP24_en.pdf

The Origins of Greece's Debt Crisis https://www.investopedia.com/articles/personal-finance/061115/origins-greeces-debt-crisis.asp#:~:text=The%20Greek%20debt%20crisis%20is,over%20the%20next%20thirty%20years

The IMF and the Greek Crisis: Myths and Realities

Speech by Poul Thomsen, Director of the European Department of the International Monetary Fund, at the London School of Economics https://www.imf.org/en/News/Articles/2019/10/01/sp093019-The-IMF-and-the-Greek-Crisis-Myths-and-Realities

Chapter 1. Fiscal Politics https://www.elibrary.imf.org/display/book/9781475547900/ch001.xml

Policy Challenges for the Next 50 Years https://www.oecd.org/economy/Policy-challenges-for-the-next-fifty-years.pdf

But Will It Work?: Implementation Analysis to Improve Government Performance R. Kent Weaver https://www.brookings.edu/wp-content/upl

oads/2016/06/02_implementation_analysis_weaver.pdf

Cross-Border Impacts of Fiscal Policy: Still Relevant? file:///C:/Users/USER/Downloads/c4.pdf

What Is a Tax Treaty Between Countries & How Does It Work? https://www.investopedia.com/terms/t/taxtreaty.asp

Five common challenges with Operational Transfer Pricing https://www.deloitte.com/global/en/services/tax/perspectives/five-common-challenges-with-operational-transfer-pricing.html

Common Transfer Pricing Issues and How to Rectify Them https://www.vietnam-briefing.com/news/transfer-pricing-issues.html/

Regional Financial Cooperation https://repositorio.cepal.org/server/api/core/bitstreams/c5982d1f-ee4a-464d-8e51-d199b48391b3/content

The Coordination of National Fiscal Policies in the Context of Monetary Union https://www.europarl.europa.eu/workingpapers/econ/pdf/e6en_en.pdf

ASEAN-5: Further Harnessing the Benefits of Regional Integration amid Fragmentation Risks file:///C:/Users/USER/Downloads/wpiea2023191-print-pdf.pdf

Base erosion and profit shifting https://en.wikipedia.org/wiki/Base_erosion_and_profit_shifting#:~:text=Base%20erosion%20and%20profit%20shifting%20(BEPS)%20refers%20to%20corporate%20tax,the%20higher%2Dtax%20jurisdictions%20using

Cap and Trade vs Carbon Tax https://earth.org/cap-and-trade-vs-carbon-tax/#:~:text=While%20a%20carbon%20tax%20sets,the%20rise%20of%20global%20temperatures.

Which is better: carbon tax or cap-and-trade? https://www.lse.ac.uk/granthaminstitute/explainers/which-is-better-carbon-tax-or-cap-and-trade/

What are some ways businesses can incentivize sustainable tourism practices? https://www.linkedin.com/advice/1/what-some-ways-businesses-can-incentivize-sustainable

Practical incentives needed to help firms adopt green practices: official https://vietnamlawmagazine.vn/practical-incentives-needed-to-help-fir

ms-adopt-green-practices-official-69852.html

Green Credit Programme of India: Incentivizing Environmental Actions and Paving the Way for a Sustainable Future https://calculuscarbon.com/green-credit-programme-of-india-incentivizing-environmental-actions-and-paving-the-way-for-a-sustainable-future/

Taxing Cryptocurrencies file:///C:/Users/USER/Downloads/wpiea2023144-print-pdf%20(1).pdf

Social impact bond https://en.wikipedia.org/wiki/Social_impact_bond#:~:text=Social%20Impact%20Bonds%20(SIBs)%20are

Social Impact Bond (SIB): Definition, How It Works, and Example https://www.investopedia.com/terms/s/social-impact-bond.asp

Green Bonds And The Emergence Of Sustainable Finance In The Nigerian Capital Market https://tnp.com.ng/insights/green-bonds-and-the-emergence-of-sustainable-finance-in-the-nigerian-capital-market

Green Bond https://corporatefinanceinstitute.com/resources/esg/green-bond/

South Korea postpones 20% tax on crypto gains to 2025 https://www.forbesindia.com/article/crypto-made-easy/south-korea-postpones-20-tax-on-crypto-gains-to-2025/78341/1

The Current State of Crypto Taxation in South Korea https://www.tekedia.com/the-current-state-of-crypto-taxation-in-south-korea/

Enhancing tax transparency with blockchain technology https://punchng.com/enhancing-tax-transparency-with-blockchain-technology/#:~:text=Blockchain%20technology%20has%20the%20potential,reducing%20tax%20evasion%20and%20fraud

How we use data and analytics https://www.ato.gov.au/about-ato/commitments-and-reporting/information-and-privacy/how-we-use-data-and-analytics

Use of Big Data in Tax Administrations https://www.ciat.org/use-of-big-data-in-tax-administrations/?lang=en

Strategic tax management: best practices help ensure competitiveness https://www.dpc.com.br/strategic-tax-management-best-practices-help-ensure-competitiveness/?lang=en

7 Ways to Maximize Tax Savings with Strategic Tax Management https://www.nidhicpa.com/7-ways-to-maximize-tax-savings-with-strategic-tax-management/

What Are Tax Management Strategies? https://www.trilogyfs.com/tax-management-strategies/

Corporate Tax Planning and Financial Performance of Development Banks in Nigeria file:///C:/Users/USER/Downloads/SSRN-id3896368.pdf

Navigating the Nuances: Tax Planning with Legal Precision and Ethical Integrity https://www.linkedin.com/pulse/navigating-nuances-tax-planning-legal-precision-ethical-fdxec?trk=article-ssr-frontend-pulse_more-articles_related-content-card

Tax avoidance might be legal but it's time we seriously questioned its ethics https://www.manchester.ac.uk/discover/news/tax-avoidance-legal-ethics/

What Are Some Ways to Minimize Tax Liability? https://www.investopedia.com/ask/answers/040715/what-are-some-ways-minimize-tax-liability.asp

6 Strategies to Protect Income from Taxes https://www.investopedia.com/articles/personal-finance/032116/top-6-strategies-protect-your-income-taxes.asp

Business Taxation Meaning: Everything You Need to Know https://www.upcounsel.com/business-taxation-meaning#:~:text=of%20business%20operations.-,The%20meaning%20of%20business%20taxation%20refers%20to%20the%20taxes%20that,for%20adhering%20to%20tax%20regulations

How Does Corporate Taxation Affect Business Investment? Evidence From Aggregate and Firm-Level Data https://one.oecd.org/document/ECO/WKP(2023)18/en/pdf

Taxation of Income from Business and Investment https://www.imf.org/external/pubs/nft/1998/tlaw/eng/ch16.pdf

The Tax Advantage of Big Business: How the Structure of Corporate Taxation Fuels Concentration and Inequality https://journals.sagepub.com/doi/10.117

7/0032329220911778

Corporate Tax: Definition, Deductions, How It Works https://www.investo pedia.com/terms/c/corporatetax.asp

Determining the impact of taxation on corporate financial decision-making Savina Princen https://www.cairn.info/revue-reflets-et-perspectives-de-la-vie-economique-2012-3-page-161.htm

Reclaiming corporate tax revenues https://www.epi.org/publication/reclai ming-corporate-tax-revenues/

Tax Planning For Beginners: 6 Key Principles Explained https://www.botk eeper.com/blog/tax-planning-for-beginners-6-key-principles-explained

The Principles of Proactive Tax Planning [Five Considerations for Business Owners] https://warrenaverett.com/insights/the-principles-of-proactive-tax-planning-five-considerations-for-business-owners/

Four Reasons to Align Your Supply Chain and Tax Strategies https://www.b do.com/insights/tax/four-reasons-to-align-your-supply-chain-and-tax-strategies

How do you balance risk and reward in decision making? https://www.link edin.com/advice/0/how-do-you-balance-risk-reward-decision-making

Balancing risk and reward: How C-suite leaders can innovate responsibly https://www.fastcompany.com/90977835/balancing-risk-and-reward-ho w-c-suite-leaders-can-innovate-responsibly

Tax Planning Process https://www.stptax.com/tax-planning/tax-plannin g-process/

What is tax planning? https://www.dsaprospect.co.uk/guides/tax-plannin g

Tax planning process https://taxfitness.com.au/tax-planning/tax-planni ng-process/

4-step process for tax planning https://www.farmprogress.com/manage ment/4-step-process-for-tax-planning

Tax Credit vs. Deduction: What's the Difference? Both reduce your tax bill—but in different ways https://www.wsj.com/buyside/personal-finance/ tax-credit-vs-deduction-6f611898

Tax Deductions & Credits https://www.investopedia.com/tax-deductions-

and-credits-4689689

What Is Tax Avoidance and How Is It Different From Tax Evasion? https://www.investopedia.com/terms/t/tax_avoidance.asp

Minimize taxes and maximize your bottom line https://www.investopedia.com/articles/stocks/11/intro-tax-efficient-investing.asp

Tax-Exempt Interest Definition and Examples https://www.investopedia.com/terms/t/taxexemptinterest.asp

Retirement Contribution: Meaning, Types, Limits https://www.investopedia.com/terms/r/retirement-contribution.asp

Tax Break Definition, Different Types, How to Get One https://www.investopedia.com/terms/t/tax-break.asp

How to get the most money back on your tax return https://www.investopedia.com/financial-edge/0312/how-to-get-the-most-money-back-on-your-tax-return.aspx

Tax Credit: What It Is, How It Works, What Qualifies, 3 Types https://www.investopedia.com/terms/t/taxcredit.asp

23 Income Tax Incentives for Investment https://www.imf.org/external/pubs/nft/1998/tlaw/eng/ch23.pdf

Understanding Business Expenses and Which Are Tax Deductible https://www.investopedia.com/terms/b/businessexpenses.asp

Deductible vs. Non-deductible Business Expenses https://www.sorgecpa.com/resources/insights/deductible-vs.-non-deductible-business-expenses

Ordinary and Necessary Expense: What it is, How it Works https://www.investopedia.com/terms/o/oandne.asp

Amortization vs. Depreciation: What's the Difference? https://www.investopedia.com/ask/answers/06/amortizationvsdepreciation.asp#:~:text=Amortization%20and%20depreciation%20are%20two,to%20reflect%20its%20anticipated%20deterioration

Amortization vs. Depreciation: What's the Difference? https://www.investopedia.com/ask/answers/06/amortizationvsdepreciation.asp#:~:text=Amortization%20and%20depreciation%20are%20two,to%20reflect%20its%20anticipated%20deterioration

R&D Tax Credits and Deductions https://pro.bloombergtax.com/brief/rdtax-credit-and-deducting-rd-expenditures/

Renewable Energy Credits (RECs), Explained https://watchwire.ai/renewa ble-energy-credits-recs-explained/#:~:text=So%2C%20What%20Exactly %20Are%20Renewable,power%20lines%20that%20transport%20energy.

Navigating the World of Taxation: A Comprehensive Guide https://www.lin kedin.com/pulse/navigating-world-taxation-comprehensive-guide#:~:tex t=Intriguingly%2C%20the%20considerations%20of%20residency,shape% 20the%20international%20tax%20landscape

Transfer Pricing: What It Is and How It Works, With Examples https://ww w.investopedia.com/terms/t/transfer-pricing.asp

International Tax Planning and Compliance https://www.hco.com/insights/ international-tax-planning-and-compliance

Guidance Note Compliance Risk Management: Managing and Improving Tax Compliance https://www.oecd.org/tax/administration/33818656.pdf

How Tax Treaties Prevent Tax Leakage in Cross-Border Projects https://w ww.huntonak.com/en/insights/how-tax-treaties-prevent-tax-leakage-in- cross-border-projects.html

Improving Tax Compliance: Establishing a Risk Management Framework https://www.adb.org/publications/improving-tax-compliance

Internal Audit and Tax Compliance https://myusf.usfca.edu/internal-audit

Internal Control System and Tax Compliance: An Empirical Analysis https://www.ijicc.net/images/vol11iss12/111204_Prawira_2020_E_R.pdf

Navigating Tax Risks in Indirect Tax: A Strategic Guide for Risk Management https://www.complyiq.io/navigating-tax-risks/

The promise and limitations of information technology for tax mobilization https://blogs.worldbank.org/developmenttalk/promise-and-limitations-i nformation-technology-tax-mobilization

Information Technology for Tax Administration https://pdf.usaid.gov/pdf_ docs/pnaea485.pdf

5 Tax Planning Examples https://www.modwm.com/5-tax-planning-exa mples/

4 global tax trends and how they impact your operations https://www.tm

f-group.com/en/news-insights/articles/2019/april/global-tax-trend-and-impact-your-operations/

About the Author

Professor Uwem Essia is a distinguished academic and celebrated author known for his illustrious career in leadership, management, economics, and development. Since June 2021, Professor Essia has immersed himself in personal studies and established himself as a prolific online book publisher, with a presence on platforms. He holds a PhD degree in Economics. Professor Uwem Essia's career is a testament to his passion for knowledge, education, and the betterment of society. His vast experience, research contributions, and dedication to fostering positive change make him a prominent figure in leadership, management, and economics. With a wealth of knowledge and a commitment to academic excellence, Professor Essia continues to make a significant impact. He is open to collaboration in joint research work/consulting, Adjunct and remote teaching, theses/dissertation supervision, professorial assessment, article/book editing and previewing, and joint book and article publishing.

You can connect with me on:

🌐 https://digitalgainspro.com

📘 https://www.facebook.com/uwem.essia.3

🔗 https://www.amazon.com/author/uwemessia

Also by Uwem Essia

Cryptoization, It Solutions, and Taxation for Sustainable Development: Digital Dynamics and Fiscal Strategies in a Transforming World

CRYPTOIZATION, IT SOLUTIONS, AND TAXATION FOR SUSTAINABLE DEVELOPMENT is a captivating exploration of financial innovation, unveiling complexities in crypto asset taxation, strategic IT decision-making, and the synergy of smart contracts, AI/ML, and finance. This book delivers profound insights, from challenges posed by cryptocurrency and AI/ML adoption to green fiscal reforms and the choice of IT tools to deploy. With strategic perspectives, case studies, and future trajectories, the author contributes to the evolving discourse on digital dynamics and the evolution of fiscal strategies in a fast-transforming world. The book is useful for academics and practitioners in taxation management, fiscal policies, and green financial innovations, among other sustainable development areas.

Fiscalization, Internal Control, and Optimal Tax Compliance: Building a Resilient Tax Compliance Ecosystem

The book "Fiscalization, Internal Control, and Optimal Tax Compliance" is the fifth of the Series titled Public Finance, Fiscal Policy and Tax Management. It explores the strategic nexus of internal controls, tax compliance, fiscalization, and broader organizational objectives. Navigate the landscape of compliance risk management, where comprehensive strategies, data management, and long-term viability considerations converge. Uncover the strategic dimensions of taxpayer compliance enhancement, from understanding root causes to fostering trust. Embark on a journey through strategic frameworks, annual compliance programs, and effective evaluation methodologies. Conclude with a transformative exploration of electronic fiscal reporting, illuminating the role of technology in shaping tax compliance. A comprehensive guide empowering individuals and organizations on the path to optimal tax compliance excellence.

ECONOMIC GOVERNANCE AND PUBLIC FINANCE DYNAMICS: Public Expenditure Policy and the Path to Sustainable Development

"Economic Governance and Public Finance Dynamics" is the third book of the Series, Public Finance, Fiscal Policy and Tax Management, wherein the author dissects issues of public expenditure policy, public goods, fiscal policies, and fiscal federalism. Each chapter navigates a crucial facet of economic governance linked to fiscal policies' multifaceted nature, exploring the dynamics of debt financing and illuminating the profound impact of public investments on economic development. It offers a comprehensive understanding of economic landscapes, with insights from renowned scholars. The book is a useful intellectual resource for academics and practitioners working on government budget preparation and implementation, economic development planning, and public-private partnerships.

www.ingramcontent.com/pod-product-compliance
Lightning Source LLC
Chambersburg PA
CBHW071048290526
45795CB00004B/1391